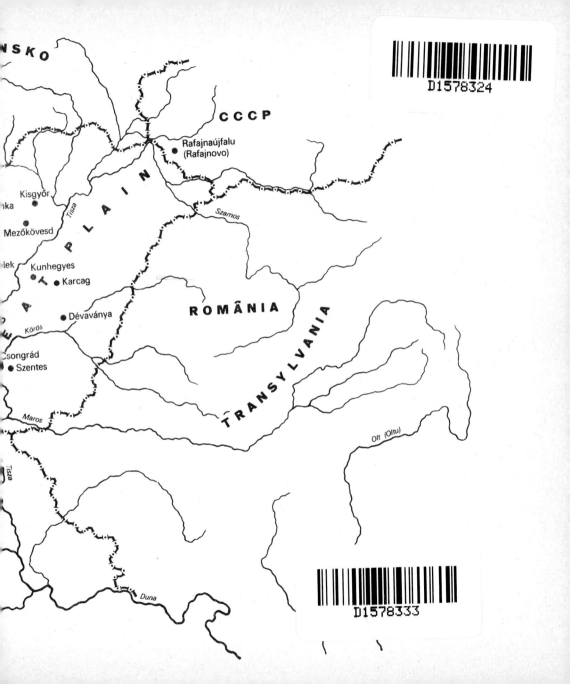

HUNGARIAN FOLK ART
Editor: Gyula Ortutay

Contents

HUNGARIAN FOLK SONGS AND FOLK INSTRUMENTS

by János Manga

Corvina

Title of the Hungarian original: Magyar népdalok, népi hangszerek
Corvina Kiadó, 1969
Translated by Gyula Gulyás
Translation revised by Cynthia Jolly and David Skuse
Cover design by Julianna Rácz
Map by Gyula Gáll
Photographs by Kata Kálmán (2) Károly Koffán (3)
and from the Archives of the Ethnographical Museum, Budapest
Colour photographs from the Birinyi Collection, Táborfalva
Cover photograph by József Faragó
Third, revised edition
© János Manga, 1969
ISBN 963 13 7443 2
ISSN 0324–7996
Printed in Hungary, 1988
Printing House, Kner 𝕏
CO 2771-h-8892

THE DISCOVERY OF FOLK SONGS

*"Each folk tune is a model of high artistic perfection.
I regard folk songs as masterworks in miniature, as I do
Bach fugues, or Mozart sonatas within the world of the
larger forms."*
                                    Béla Bartók

The rise of nationalism, that tremendous intellectual force which galvanized Europe during the late 18th and 19th centuries, reached Hungary relatively early on, and inspired an exploration of its unique heritage. In Hungary the essence of this heritage was believed to lie in its folk poetry, music and customs. A renewed intellectual life, and a flowering of national culture were expected to result from research into these traditions.

These aspirations began to mature in the 1760s, and in the following decades met with an ever-increasing response. In the interests of national progress, the Hungarian poet György Bessenyei (1747–1811) championed the use of Hungarian in the nation's literature, the development of a strong educational system, a national utilization of every human faculty, and the need to harness science.★ In his complaint that the aristocracy just roamed abroad, unaware of the treasures preserved by the Hungarian peasantry, he was opposing the obsolete feudalistic culture of his time, and even his own class. In 1782, Miklós Révai (1760–1807), a worthy follower of György Bessenyei and his associates, wrote an enthusiastic appeal to the *Magyar Hírmondó* (Hungarian Courier), urging that old songs, sung in the language of the people, be collected. The aim was to acquaint the public with Hungarian as a language, and with its differences of dialect. His appeal was not in vain.

Hungarian poets turned with an ever growing interest to folk poetry, and men such as Ferenc Faludi (1704–1779), Mihály Csokonai Vitéz (1773–1805), and Sándor Petőfi (1823–1849) made collections of folk song texts. The simplicity and beauty of these texts profoundly influenced their own poetry. The poet János Arany wrote: "I can well understand that even a poet such as Petőfi—as I often heard him say—would have been happy if the bulk of his own poetry had been as beautiful as some of our folk songs." In 1803 Csokonai told his friends to listen carefully to the singing of the village girl and the simple grape-picker. That same year, Benedek

★ Hungarian had been declining over the course of the 18th century; Vienna naturally encouraged the use of German in official matters, whilst the Hungarian nobility used Latin.

Virág (1754–1830) wrote to Ferenc Kazinczy, describing how one evening, while smoking his pipe by the window, he heard a clear voice singing: "What is the use of coming to you, my love?" He heard no more because of a sudden disturbance, and wanted Kazinczy to send the song to him if it was known in his part of the country, together with any other amusing or comical songs.

The writer and editor István Kultsár (1760–1828) urged that a collection of the unsophisticated songs of common people be published in the *Hasznos Mulattató* (Useful Entertainer), for it was through these songs that Hungarian national characteristics could best be understood. Ferenc Kölcsey (1790–1838), the author of the *Himnusz* (the poem that became the text of the Hungarian national anthem), expressed the same view when he wrote in 1826: "The sparks of true national poetry are to be found in the songs of the common people."

Early in the 19th century (1813) Ádám Pálóczi Horváth completed his manuscript-collection of 360 melodies: *Ó és Új, mint egy ötödfélszázad énekek* (Four-and-a-half-hundred Tunes, Old and New). Zoltán Kodály has pointed out that Pálóczi Horváth was not a true folk song collector, but wanted a written record of the songs he knew. Nevertheless, his book which contains ancient folk songs, more recent art songs, foreign tunes and church hymns, as well as some he had composed himself, added fuel to the flames flaring up ever more frequently in Hungarian life. The attempts at repression made by the Habsburg Court in Vienna had the effect of emphasizing Hungarian national consciousness, which increasingly found its inspiration in Hungarian history and folk poetry. In 1831 and 1832 Esztergom and Komárom Counties addressed a petition to the Hungarian Academy of Sciences, requesting that it publish folk songs. The Academy issued an appeal for folk songs to be collected, as a result of which the General Secretary, Mihály Vörösmarty, the poet, received ten note-books in 1833, containing about a thousand songs. The Academy handed them over to the Kisfaludy Society, and from there they went into the possession of János Erdélyi. A collection, still in manuscript, *Áriák és Dalok* (Arias and Songs) by the Protestant choirmaster István Tóth of Fülöpszállás, is a considerable source for this period. Written between 1832 and 1843, it contains numerous folk songs. Hungarian folk songs also attracted the attention of Ferenc Liszt. It was his intention to wander on foot through some of the most remote regions of Hungary with a knapsack, but, according to a letter of 1838, nothing ever came of his plans.

The collection and publication of folk material—texts for the most part—began in a limited way around the middle of the last century. In 1846, the Kisfaludy Society announced a competition for the collection of folk songs, folk tales and customs. János Erdélyi's two-volume work *Népdalok és Mondák* (Folk Songs and Legends) was published between 1846 and 1848. Its preface reflected its author's intentions: "Travelling through Germany, I had ample opportunity to speak with men of science, who were pleased to inquire about the Hungarian race. Whenever the conversation touched upon its small population, I was never asked about its politics, but whether it had its own manner of attire, songs, dances and traditional customs." About this time János Erdélyi published a small collection entitled *Magyar Népdalok Énekre és Zongorára* (Hungarian Folk Songs for Voice and Piano)—the result of a commission by the Kisfaludy Society. In 1863, there appeared János Kriza's collection of texts entitled *Vadrózsák* (Wild Roses). In this collection art song texts patterned on folk models turn up side by side with folk poetry, and there is a separate chapter dedicated to songs in folk music style, contributed by various authors. In his preface, Kriza also noted how the nation had been rejuvenated through folk poetry: "The reawakened soul of the nation probed more deeply within itself, to fortify and consolidate its own national being against destructive calamity, nourishing itself on folk elements to give itself shape and colour."

The Kisfaludy Society's appeal and János Erdélyi's two-volume collection evoked nationwide response and stimulated enthusiastic collectors in different parts of the country. In 1865, Gyula Pap published a volume entitled *Palóc Népköltemények* (Palóc Folk Poems). This contained folk songs, folk tales, riddles, and children's games collected in the region of Salgótarján. In the foreword of his small volume, he gave a brief ethnographical description of the large Palóc families, discussing spinning, folk costumes, and marriage. Of the music he wrote: "The older men seldom sing, and even the young men do so only when they pledge a toast, or work alone in the fields. The women, on the other hand, never work without a song. They are very fond of sad songs; their melodies are not varied to any great extent, but are drawnout. Yet they are quite unsurpassed in the expression of feelings and in creating an effect." Pap was quite clear about the importance of uniting text and tune: "What a great service the Kisfaludy Society could perform for our national music, if it insisted on having the tunes of the various localities notated!... In folk music the tune is so closely knit with the text that one cannot be analysed without the other."

Once the importance of linking tune and text had been established, collections in the second half of the century began to appear with the tunes. The most noteworthy of these were Károly Szini's *A magyar nép dalai és dallamai* (Songs and Melodies of the Hungarian People),

1865; István Bartalus's *Magyar népdalok egyetemes gyűjteménye* (Universal Collection of Hungarian Folk Songs), volumes I–VII, 1837–1896; and, Áron Kiss's *Magyar gyermekjátékgyűjtemény* (Collection of Hungarian Children's Games), 1891. These publications were influential in their time and milestones in the history of folk music research. However, apart from Áron Kiss's collection, their authors were still unable to differentiate between folk songs and art songs, some of which were composed in folk music style. Nor was the notation always satisfactory. Béla Bartók judged only 130 of the 200 tunes in Szini's collection to be of peasant origin. He found 411 peasant songs in Bartalus's seven volumes, 32 of them borrowed from Szini's collection. Bartók described Szini's notation as passable—Szini was not a trained musician—and that of Bartalus as more defective.

A new era in Hungarian folk music research emerged around the turn of the century. Beginning field work in 1896, Béla Vikár became the first *systematic* collector of Hungarian folk music. He made use of the Edison phonograph because he did not consider his musical training adequate for recording text and music *(Plates 3 and 4.)* He recorded 1,492 songs on 875 cylinders, the greater part of which was later transcribed by Béla Bartók and Zoltán Kodály. *(Plates 1 and 2.)* It was, in fact, Vikár's cylinders that induced the two young musicians in 1905 to concentrate on folk music research.

Bartók wrote of this in his autobiography: "In my studies of folk music I discovered that what we had known as Hungarian folk songs till then were more or less trivial songs by popular composers and did not contain much that was valuable. I felt an urge to go deeper into this question and set out in 1905 to collect and study Hungarian peasant music unknown until then. It was my great good luck to find a helpmate for this work in Zoltán Kodály, who, owing to his deep insight and sound judgement in all spheres of music, could give me many hints and much advice that proved of immense value."

In a short time marvellous results were born of this splendid co-operation. By the early 1920s, nearly 8,000 songs had been collected, a great part of them by Bartók and Kodály. Later, they were joined by László Lajtha and a group of younger collectors, and the quantity of material continued to grow. Towards the end of the 1930s, the Folk Music Collection of the Ethnographical Museum had in its custody 3,500 cylinders and 155 grpm records. The Folk Music Research Group of the Hungarian Academy of Sciences was founded in 1953. This group augmented the Collection by about 45,000 songs, developed melodic cataloguing systems, and compiled the huge volumes of the *Corpus Musicae Popularis Hungaricae.*

The character of "the unknown folk music of Hungary" was examined from a fresh perspective by Bartók and Kodály. In his book, *Hungarian Folk Music,* published in Hungarian in 1924, in German in 1925, and in English in 1931, Bartók wrote: "The term 'peasant music' connotes, broadly speaking, all the tunes which endure among the peasant class of any nation, in a more or less wide area and for a more or less long period, and which constitute a spontaneous expression of the musical feeling of that class... Taken in narrower sense, peasant music is the sum total of the tunes belonging to one or several, more or less homogeneous styles." In his work on the folk music of Hungarian and neighbouring peoples, Bartók modified this definition as follows: "Folk music is the sum total of all the tunes in use in a community, the spontaneous expression of its musical instinct over a given area, for a certain period of time. Put more simply, it is made up of tunes sung by many people over a long period." Bartók describes how tunes undergo changes and form variants. "On the other hand, tunes that originally differed from one another develop similarities, so that a homogeneous style of melody emerges. The co-existence of a great number of tunes more or less resembling one another is a characteristic trait of folk music."

Zoltán Kodály's study, "Folk Music of Hungary", was the second major work to appear. It was included in the fourth volume of *A Magyarság Néprajza* (Hungarian Ethnography) in 1937, and was later published as a separate study. Kodály was not so much concerned with what constitutes a folk song as with the question, "What do peasants sing?" He showed how differentiations in peasant society were reflected in its musical life, concluding: "Folk tradition should not be thought of as one uniform, homogeneous whole. Profound differences appear according to age, social and material conditions, religion, cultural level, region, and sex... Village society is uniform only when viewed from a distance. The more closely it is studied, the more gradations of difference appear. There are differences resulting from occupations (tradesman, farmer, servant, herdsman), and from property and religion among people of identical occupation. They are shown in the songs they know." Hence Kodály's answer to "What is folk song? What is it that people sing?" is to point out the complex relationship between the folk song and village social life, thereby revealing the rich and varied melodic world which still characterizes the musical life of Hungarian peasants.

ANCIENT HERITAGE
AND LIVING FOLK SONGS

Although its results soon compensated the two young musicologists for their arduous work, the regular research which began in 1905 was fraught with difficulty. Béla Bartók later wrote about this time: "To discover musical material untouched by civilization, we had to seek out villages remote from urban centres and lines of communication. In those days there were still a great many such villages in Hungary. If we wanted to hear older songs, some several hundred years old, we had to turn to old people, especially to the older women; but it was difficult to persuade them to sing... In a word, we had to live under the most primitive conditions, in the most miserable villages, and to concentrate on winning the friendship and confidence of the peasants. This later was hard to achieve; the nobility has so exploited the peasants that they were mistrustful of anyone who appeared to belong to the 'gentry'. All the same, our toils gave me much pleasure. The happiest days of my life were those which I spent in villages, amongst peasants."

The folk music material collected by the two young researchers revealed melodic forms which have preserved the ancient musical heritage of the Hungarian people. "At the beginning of this century," wrote Bartók, "only old people and particularly old women knew the old-style tunes. But, even though they remembered them and sang a great number quite authentically, only rarely could they be heard singing them—they could not be heard when they were working, nor at home after work, nor in periods of relaxation... Even if several singers happened to know the same songs, they were reluctant to sing together, and their performances differed so greatly with respect to ornamentation, that we could not even begin to have them sing in chorus."

Zoltán Kodály described this ancient heritage as follows: "The five-note scale was the starting-point for the music of many ancient peoples, and possibly of every people: it lives and flourishes amongst us too, as we have realized since 1907, when Béla Bartók first found such tunes in great quantity in the Székely region." From Bartók's and Kodály's comparative studies, it became apparent that this stratum of Hungarian folk music, thriving not only amongst the Székelys but also in other parts of the country, had survived from the era of ancient Hungarian history (before the settlement in the Danube basin by 896 A.D.) Although tunes always undergo changes, they preserve their basic characteristics for hundreds and thousands of years. Because of this, comparative research can shed light on the history of folk songs, from their origin through the time when they become the property of certain groups of people. Five-note tunes of related type survive amongst those kindred peoples with whom Hungarians lived in cultural, linguistic and musical community during their early history.

Like the language, this ancient stratum of Hungarian folk music was so much a part of peasant consciousness that nothing could cause it to be forgotten or pushed into the background, not even the migrations, nor the large number of alien influences surrounding the peasantry in their new country. Despite the fact that over the course of long centuries this ancient heritage changed, took on different forms, and assumed a more modern garb, almost exact variants of several extant tune-types are to be found in the music of peoples speaking languages related to Hungarian living in the Soviet Union, in Cheremissian music in particular, as well as in Turkish folk music. As Zoltán Kodály wrote: "The path followed by Hungarian music was bound to be the same as that of the Hungarian language and people. Wherever the people wandered and multiplied, their music went with them. Whatever influenced their language must have influenced their music, too... Today the Magyars represent the outermost edge of the great Asiatic musical tradition, many thousands of years old, which is rooted in the spirit of the various peoples living from China, through Central Asia, to the Black Sea." Bartók also pointed out the common Central Asian source of ancient Hungarian and Turkish folk music.

Once Hungarian linguists had confirmed that Hungarian had a Finno-Ugrian origin, it was logical to assume that Hungarian folk music, too, preserved Finno-Ugric elements. As early as 1933, Bence Szabolcsi established a method of folk music research which promised to recover part of this Finno-Ugrian heritage. Subsequent research has revealed that such elements exist, not in complete four-line folk songs, but in *regös* (minstrel) songs with their reiterated motifs, in laments with pattern variations, and more recently, in dance-tunes known as *ungaresca*. These types, however, fall outside the category of folk songs and are therefore not discussed in detail here.

Zoltán Kodály first described the characteristics of pentatonic tunes in his study "The Five-

11

Note Scale in Hungarian Folk Music", published in 1917. A detailed analysis followed in his work *Folk Music of Hungary*, in 1937. This ancient stratum of Hungarian folk melody is characterized by the pentatonic (five-note) scale, and a melodic structure that is transposed down a fifth (five notes lower). As the name indicates, the pentatonic scale consists of only five notes. In essence it differs from the European heptatonic (seven-note major or minor) scale in that the second and the sixth tones are missing. If the starting-point is taken as G^1 (a fifth above middle c or C^1) the notes of the pentatonic scale ascend as follows: G^1—B flat^1—C^2—D^2—F^2. But the missing A^1 and E^2 often occur as unaccented passing-notes. Many present–day tunes have adopted the heptatonic scale and their range is often extended: G^2, A^2 and B flat^2 may also occur.

Let us now take a look at the melodic technique of transposition down a fifth. An analysis of the two transcriptions that follow will make this matter clear. The tune is first sung using the first and second lines of the text, while the third and fourth lines of the text go with the same melody transposed. This repetition of the melody in transposition is also known as the "fifth construction":

Surd, Somogy County

Rafajnaújfalu (Rafajnovo, Soviet Union), 1912. Collected by Bartók

As these two examples show, the tempo of Hungarian pentatonic tunes is generally slow and they are sung melismatically (with more than one note per syllable). This is shown in the first example, where the crotchets, quavers, semi-quavers alternate with crotches and quavers lengthened by dots. The tempo of the second song has the faster, livelier pace of a dance tune, and consists only of quavers and crotchets of equal values. Tunes with fluctuating rhythms, that is, those sung *a tempo rubato,* as in the first example, show an abundance of ornamental notes. These ornamental notes are shown with smaller notes. With the exception of one or two regions in Hungary, only an occasional elderly singer, an old woman living alone, or an old herdsman has been heard singing in this rich, ornamental style during the last few decades. It is a kind of singing which hardly exists any more.

Generally the tunes are sung to four lines of verse with equal numbers of syllables, but there are some exceptions. The most common lines consist of 6, 7, 8, 11 and 12 syllables. In the first example, all four lines have six syllables each, but in the second example this exact four-line symmetry is lacking.

Naturally only a very few tunes have preserved this pentatonic scale and structure in its pure form. The majority have been transformed by the musical cultures that have influenced Magyar music in its new land over a thousand years. All the same, traces of this ancient heritage live on in the "new-style" folk tunes still thriving today.

It is characteristic of any folk culture that some of the older elements undergo transformation as new elements are assimilated. Older traits come to resemble what has recently been absorbed, and new forms emerge. Preserving many of the older features, new forms resemble grafted branches that bear new fruit while receiving nourishment from the old tree. The ancient tree of Hungarian past has produced new fruit in the shape of today's "new-style" folk songs.

In order to understand more clearly the circumstances which gave rise to this strikingly successful "new-style" folk song, it is necessary to examine the period following the tragic 150-year Turkish occupation. After the liberation of Buda, the Turks withdrew from the heart of the country in 1686 and the joyful news swept through Europe. But few people were aware that, in the wake of the defeated Turkish troops, there remained only scorched, plundered and deserted *pusztas* with decimated populations. The inevitable aftermath of these unusual conditions was that strangers settled in this region and the serfs wandered away. The landlords, whose serfs left the land, recruited serfs from other regions of the country. In many places, even the landlords were new, and often serfs whose mother tongue was German or Slav were settled on the estates of landlords of non-Hungarian nationality. The counties issued decree after decree in an effort to prevent migration and escape of serfs. The decrees were not very effective. The unbearable taxes, and in numerous places, the shortage of land, crop failures, the tyranny of the landlords, military billeting and pestilence drove the serfs elsewhere in pursuit of a better life.

In many regions, even the surviving population underwent change; survivors of families that had lost everything left their homes and settled elsewhere in an effort to forget their grief. Sometimes serfs only found permanent homes after the fourth or fifth try. These conditions prompted a large-scale influx of alien peoples in search of better living conditions. They either settled in established villages or founded new communities of their own. In some places they lived as isolated communities speaking their own language, while in others they merged with the Hungarian population. After a time, the culture of a particular region would begin to emerge with its own special colour, amalgamating old and new, native and alien.

The situation in the Hungarian countryside in the late 17th and early 18th centuries was made even more complex by new developments in the country's economic life. A steadily-growing differentiation arose among the serfs who comprised the village population. The large self-sufficient feudal estates were transformed into large manorial estates specializing in the production of certain commodities. These large farms were able to produce grain and breed livestock, and were often made even larger by the addition of tracts of arable land; hence, the landlord's household servants and serfs could no longer provide sufficient manpower. To fill that gap, the increasingly numerous landless cotters were employed. Thus a peasantry began to develop with a way of life and social position differing greatly from that of the serfs.

Many others of this rapidly growing class earned a living by casual work, and continued to live in the village without becoming separated from the community. But the village population still continued to include landed serfs, who enjoyed freer and better conditions. At the end of the 18th century and the first half of the 19th, their life differed substantially not only from that of tenant farmers but also from that of families farming the scattered lands held in villein tenure. Hand in hand with this economic and social development involving stratification went class movement; some families moved from the status of serfdom to become cotters, servants or herdsmen; others rose from servant, herdsman or cotter status to farmer, with a holding of land. As a result of trading goods at fairs, a closer relationship developed between the villages and the growing towns. The horizon of village life widened and its needs, views and tastes changed accordingly. All this was helped along by the increasing number of village schools, the spread of literacy, military service, and acquaintance with different regions and ethnic cultures.

Parallel developments took place in the realm of folk music. There was an intensification of influences from the music of chapels, churches, verse chronicles, song-writers and the orchestras of the aristocracy. There was also more frequent contact with the West. All this led to the forging of a new style to express changing tastes. Just as the serf's horizons expanded after his liberation from bondage, so the old-style song tree was again sprouting new blossoms as its melodic range was extended. This change gave a brighter colour to laborious weekdays and festive occasions alike, and inspired singing groups.

In Bartók's view these refreshing melodies, their vigorous rhythms reflecting a changing self-awareness, were much closer to the spirit of the times than the ancient tunes, which were sometimes melancholic and often alien in mood. He wondered whether any other country or people could show such "revolutionary" manifestations in the music of its peasantry. He described it as "revolutionary" because, as he wrote, "in its contemporary guise, it seeks almost tyrannically to suppress the surviving remnants of the earlier melodies." The area over which the new style spread extended beyond the limits of the Hungarian language; it flourished equally well in Moravia, Slovakia, and Ruthenia. Bartók maintained that the spread of the new style in these regions was to a considerable extent the result of young men serving their army years in Hungarian territories, of migrant farmer's workers living every year for

Fót, Pest County, 1907. Collected by Bartók

weeks and months amongst Hungarian people, and of the increasing number of gypsy orchestras roaming the more remote regions with new-style songs in their repertoires. Moreover, it would be hard to imagine how neighbouring peoples could have avoided adapting this new, rapidly spreading style into their own folk music. The historico-social forces acting upon Hungary affected them, too. The long centuries of close proximity caused diverse folk music styles to adapt similar, even identical, forms. In regions of Slovakia and Moravia there are countless examples of variants of the new style, more or less similar to their Hungarian counterparts.

Bartók attributed the closed, architectonic structure of new-style tunes to Western European influences. "Although the new style shows an organic relationship with the old style in its rhythms (and to some extent in its melodic patterns), its tunes are quite different in character because of their essentially different construction. This method of melody-building was undoubtedly established by the influence of Western forms but further development has given rise to indigenous forms which differ considerably from the original Western ones." Zoltán Kodály writes, in his study of Hungarian folk music, that of a total repertoire of some 3,000 new-style songs, 1,000 are regularly performed. He maintains that nearly 800 of these have

Tempo giusto ♩=88

Ke-lét fe-lől száll egy magas pa-csirta

Ki van annak mind a két sze-me sír-va,

Szárnya alatt hoz egy rózsás le-ve-let,

Rá van írva, hogy a ba-bám nem sze-ret.

Rimóc, Nógrád County, 1955

a reprise form. The melody of the starting line is repeated, i.e., tune-lines one and four are the same. Four main types of new-style song can be distinguished, depending on the melodic content of each of the four lines. These can be shown in letters, as follows: AA⁵A⁵A, ABBA, AA⁵BA, and AABA. In the first example, the tune-lines are all alike, except that the second and third are five notes higher. In the second type, the first and last lines are the same, but the second line is different, and is repeated in the third line. In the next example, the first and last lines are identical, the second repeats the first five notes higher, and the third is different. In the fourth type the first, second and last lines are identical, and only the third differs. To illustrate, here are four songs: the first shows type AA⁵A⁵A, the second ABBA, the third AA⁵BA and the fourth AABA.

There are a great many similarities in these songs; in fact, their texts have often been interchanged. Yet divergencies occur even amongst adjacent types, and a great richness of variants is characteristic of each type. Kodály illustrates this with a quantity of examples, and Bence Szabolcsi explains the development in terms of history. Both of them show the role of Western influences, and at the same time confirm that the new style possesses links with the structures of the old. While it is true that many of the songs make use of the seven-note scales—Do-

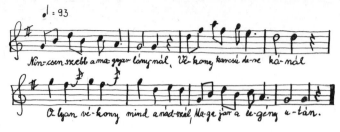

Bácsandrásszállás, Bács-Kiskun County, 1942

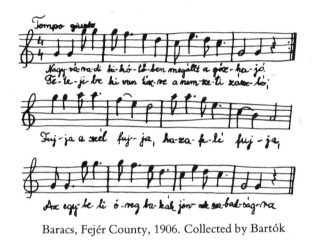

Baracs, Fejér County, 1906. Collected by Bartók

Bolhás, Somogy County, 1922. Collected by Kodály

rian, Aeolian, Mixolydian, Lydian and the modern major scale—a pure form of pentatonic scale also occurs, or a form containing only one or two extraneous notes.

We find the robust vitality of the people in every song representative of the new style. It is the vitality springing from the faith of a serf anxious to build a new world and hoping for a better way of life. He works amid the desolation caused by the 150-year Turkish occupation to rebuild the churches, the feudal castles, and the poor village hovels in the plundered, burnt and depopulated villages. The new style sprang from this same robust vitality, drawing its nourishment from the past, holding its own against more modern and alien styles. It was able to assimilate, adapt, transform and reshape the new to its own image, to create out of bewildering diversity a homogeneous new style. "As soon as a new song comes into existence, it rushes through the entire land like wildfire: neither hills, nor rivers, nor distance can impede its progress," wrote Bartók. In this way a melodic style came into being which has been essential to the musical world of the Hungarian peasantry for centuries.

LIFE OF THE FOLK SONG

Opportunities for singing have always been closely connected with the peasant way of life, with traditional customs, with certain types of work, and in many ways these determine the existence of the folk song. *(Plates 27, 29, 30* and *32).* Changes in the mode of living, the types of work and folk customs can all influence the life of the folk song, and can even result in its decline and disappearance. But closely connected with changes in the way of life are new influences bringing about new needs and new tastes. Naturally, changes can also take place when there is no essential change in the way of life, but merely in the circumstances which govern traditional observances.

The previous chapter described how ancient pentatonic melodies can only be heard here and there from old people; young people get to know them, if at all, in singing classes, or from folk song collections. By the early part of this century the old-style songs no longer played a significant role in peasant life. The new style, on the other hand, still exists, although it is rapidly vanishing with the swift changes brought by modern society. In recent years young people increasingly prefer popular music for their social gatherings.

There is also a third important style of folk song. This consists of folk variants of non-Hungarian folk songs, popular church hymns, or music, popular songs, etc. This group includes many general folk songs, as well as those sung on special occasions. It includes diverse material in terms of ethnic and historical origin.

Apart from the folk versions of art songs, whose performance style varied according to region, the song repertoire of the peasantry at the turn of the century consisted almost exclusively of folk songs with instrumental accompaniment. The time and place of group or individual singing always depended on the age of the singer and the occasion. Elderly men and women would generally sing hymns together in church, pilgrimages and other religious occasions. They sang folk songs in groups rarely at a christening, say, or a wedding. But there were more occasions for individual singing amongst the older people, especially amongst the women. During the agricultural work of spring, summer and autumn, elderly women stayed at home looking after the children, took care of farm animals and poultry, and worked in and around the house. The feeble voice of an old woman could often be heard singing a popular hymn, a folk ballad or folk song. If a singer, young or old, is asked where she has learned a particular song, she generally answers, "From my grandmother," because in her childhood she was looked after by her grandmother, or great-grandmother, and learned her first tunes and texts as she heard them performed *(Plate 31)*. At christenings, weddings, in the spinning room, and at feather-stripping parties, solo-singing could be heard from the older generation, particularly when the singer was eager to teach young people an old, forgotten, or unknown song, or was warmly pressed by the younger ones to sing. In the last few decades it has been more and more difficult to come across old women who sing or hum at home by themselves. The basic order of family life has changed, and the continuity of the singing tradition has been disrupted.

Bartók wrote that the younger generation took eagerly to tunes in the new style, and became really enthusiastic about them. A young peasant rarely learned an old-style song, and even if he did, he never sang it. According to Bartók, another factor which favoured the spread of the new-style songs was that their strict, dance-step rhythms made them especially well suited for dancing and almost inseparable from the slow and quick *csárdás* which developed in the first half of the last century. Village gypsy bands played little else, because this was what the young people sang, and the *csárdás* was the main dance of the village *(Plates 21 and II)*. A couple of decades ago girls would gather in a circle during the break of village dances, and sing these songs. In the evenings, young men could be heard singing them up and down the streets, and on Sunday afternoons, groups of girls would dance and sing round and round in a circle to the rhythm of these songs, or clasp hands in rows as they strolled from one end of the village to the other.

We have seen how the new-style song flowered as a result of opportunities for casual labour. Before 1848, the serfs were often compelled to work for feudal lords. Later on, casual labour became widely available on manorial estates: a great demand arose in sugar-beet growing, for instance, for young workers, especially for girls and young married women. Communal hoeing was accompanied by singing, which often continued in the rest periods. Hay-gathering, the grain harvest, threshing, maize picking, husking, and, in the winter months, spinning and feather-plucking were all occasions for group singing.

Some of these activities, such as spinning, have vanished long ago. Group occupations

Szék (Sic, Rumania), 1940. Collected by László Lajtha

have also changed in nature, and there was a shift in the age of the participants. Recently the pattern of rural life has undergone dramatic changes: cooperative farming provides a totally different work environment. Movie theatres and village cultural centres have created new entertainment opportunities. Gipsy orchestras, a growing number of small dance-bands, radio and television are taking the latest popular tunes to even the most remote villages. In the last few years even the new-style folk song has inevitably lost much of its life and vigour.

In his work on the Hungarian folk song, Béla Bartók assumed that the "primitive state" quite likely knew only a single category of song. He considered that the other, sharply differentiated, categories came into existence for special occasions at a later stage of development. In analysing the old and the new styles of peasant music, he really dealt only with lyrical song and ballad texts with their related dance tunes, none of them linked with special occasions. Bartók included in a third group, which he called "other Hungarian peasant tunes", the occasional tunes which did not belong musically amongst either old-style or new-style tunes. Even today this category contains many unexplained problems, although Bartók himself became convinced that many of its types were very ancient. It is not our intention here to analyze these songs of extremely mixed origin, which include tune-types borrowed at random from many sources; but it is essential to describe their social function if a true picture is to be presented.

Is-ten légyen hozzad, é-dös kedves a-pam,

Tö - led meg kell vál - nom.

I- de-gön föld, i-de - gen or-szag,

Fo- gadj en-göm hox-zad.

Jásztelek, Szolnok County

One could easily imagine that Hungarian folk music consists of only "old style" and "new-style" melodies. This, however, is not the case. In addition to these songs, Hungarian peasants sing countless others with Hungarian texts whose tunes are either of unknown or authentically foreign origin, but have been transformed to conform to the "new style". For centuries, some of these have quite likely formed part of the Hungarian folk heritage.

Another powerful influence, as a matter of course, was that of church music. This was particularly evident in many tunes connected with special occasions and feast-day ceremonies. Here and there it is possible to come across the original form of a tune long ago borrowed and adapted into a characteristically Hungarian style. But this need not give cause for wonder. The Magyars came into contact with the melodies of the Christian Church by the 8th and 9th centuries, while they were settled in the Caucasus and the Black Sea. Later, in their new home, when they had adopted the Christian faith, church liturgy and liturgical melody became part of their way of life. According to contemporary chronicles, in some villages the clergy's main aim in teaching the community was to train singers to read and understand Latin, and to act as altar boys. On feast-days, pupils went from house to house bearing greetings, and in the Middle Ages on such occasions they sang church hymns with Latin texts (later Hungarian texts). In many places this practice survived into the second half of the nineteenth century.

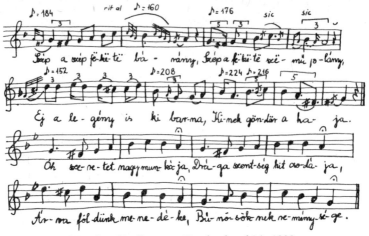

Menyhe, (Podhorany, Czechoslovakia), 1938

It was not rare to find songs sometimes sung with sacred texts, and sometimes with secular ones. And it was no wonder that in the course of many centuries the borderline between sacred and secular became blurred, and sacred music left its imprint on the secular. It became a part of everyday life, either through the folk assimilation of tunes originally belonging to the church repertoire or by the opposite process of the Church adapting for its used tunes of Hungarian origin. In the latter case, folk tunes long ago acquired religious texts, surviving to our own day in the form of folk hymns.

Tunes originally attached to ritual customs were later performed for events associated with family life, public holidays and seasonal periods of work.

The most significant ceremony associated with family life is, of course, marriage and the wedding celebration; this evoked the richest supply of melody *(Plate I)*. In certain regions, special songs were developed to correspond to every stage of the wedding. The singing of suitable songs would last from the first formal act of betrothal until the final wedding celebrations, so that the whole marriage was virtually an opera. The betrothal was celebrated in song. Singing would accompany bringing of the bride's bed and trousseau to the bridegroom's house; the escorting of the couple to the wedding and back, the bride's leaving of her parents; and the bride's dance.

24

The recent corpus of melodic material for weddings may include an occasional old-style tune, many new-style ones, and songs of other origin, including festive hymn-like songs containing secular and sacral texts. A song about the wedding of Cana of Galilee was widely used, generally sung by the guests at the wedding-feast. A few years ago it was still possible to hear how a hymn-tune had become newly linked to a secular text appropriate to the wedding dinner, but previously sung to another tune (Music Ex. No. 10).

Naturally, tunes linked to special occasions did not last for ever. A tune might last scores of years, even centuries, to be forgotten within a single generation. It might become superfluous, because the occasion with which it was connected had ceased to exist.

As to the annual holidays, Christmas was pre-eminent with its rich heritage of song material. "At Christmas time the village resounded with carols," said one of our informants. In Nativity plays, the sung and spoken texts alternated with each other *(Plate 28)*. Certain districts still kept up the old custom of house-to-house carol-singing by adults on Christmas Eve. On the evening of Christmas Day, the village streets echoed with the singing of children who, just like the grown-ups, went from house to house, singing pastoral songs borrowed from Nativity plays, Christmas hymns learnt from hymnals, and carols surviving only in folk memory. Hungarian Christmas carols, like Christmas customs, are linked by strong ties to the analogous material of their neighbours, but over the centuries they have acquired a specifically Hungarian spirit, just as the robust humour of the Hungarian peasant breaks out in the texts of pastoral songs (Music Ex. No. 11).

Drégelypalánk,
Nógrád County, 1952

25

Galambok, Zala County, 1940

Even in recent years, minstrelsy *(regölés)* was still practised here and there in Transdanubia. Young boys, and in some places teenage boys and young married men, would call at the houses of highly marriageable girls, and recite their best wishes. They carried sticks with jingling chains, mugs covered with hide, and other improvised instruments. When they came into a house, they would usually sing a few bars of a limited-range children's game song announcing themselves through the song text as "servants of King Stephen", or they sang of the mythical stag of Hungarian folklore. The main emphasis was always on the expression of good wishes and the matching of the girls to certain young men.

The Balázs and Gregory processions went out of favour at the turn of the century. In them school children would collect gifts by singing variants of songs honoured by centuries of school tradition.

The monotony of winter was broken not only by feasts at carnival time, but also by the social gatherings of young people, events with singing and dancing. Spinnery dances used to be held on Carnival Sundays, when the old spinneries still existed, and elsewhere there were parties where young people learned to dance. Carnival Sunday marked the beginning of a three-day dance festival which included humorous processions, the collecting of bacon, sausages and eggs, and the initiation of lads to manhood. At such times, the village naturally resounded with song; the older people made merry at home with wine, and the young people attended carnival balls. Throughout the country, it was an age-old custom for the musician of the carnival dance to be a bagpiper, and during the dance, young people sang gaily to the sound of the bagpipe. In the course of the dancing, the simple bagpipe tunes acquired new verses, as well as new variants on the existing texts and melodies. Gypsy orchestras came to replace the bagpipers at carnivals, and bagpipe songs only survived in the memory of the old people. The gypsy orchestras brought with them the new-style folk songs and folk versions of urban art songs.

On Sunday afternoons in spring, the singing games of the girls could be heard all over the village. On Palm Sunday the girls carried the dummy. This consisted of a procession in which the girls made a straw dummy, dressed it up as a young bride, carried it through the village, then threw it into the river, or burnt it *(Plates 23 and 24)*. The ancient melody they used for the text was similar to a children's game song. But at the turn of the century, when more and more villagers travelled to the capital to find work on large construction sites, they took home the songs they had learned in Budapest, and, in some cases, the old songs for carrying the dummy were replaced by tunes currently popular in the city. In some villages, this custom lasted until just a couple of years ago.

Ghymes (Jelenec, Czechoslovakia), 1937

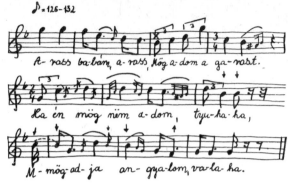

Nemespátró, Somogy County

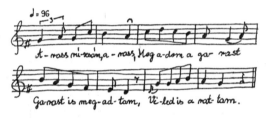

Vicsápapáti (Vyčapy–Opatovce, Czechoslovakia), 1938

Felsőiregh, Tolna County, 1907. Collected by Bartók

Later in the year, special songs were performed for the folk customs of May Day, Whitsun and Midsummer Day (St. Ivan's Day) *(Plate 26)*. In certain regions of the country, the young men put up maypoles for girls on May Day; in other places, they set them up on the Whitsun holiday. The lads would then celebrate with songs. On Whitsunday there was a traditional procession for the Whitsuntide Queen *(Plate 25)*. The girls went singing round the village, receiving gifts from each house. On Midsummer Eve, or on the day itself, boys and girls jumped over a fire and matchmaking songs were sung. The singing had to last long enough, for all the boys and girls present to participate. Thus there arose a popular saying, "Long as a song of St. Ivan". This custom began to die out in the second half of the nineteenth century, but in a few regions survived until quite recently. There were new-style, foreign derived and "flower" songs, as well as litany-like melodic fragments reminiscent of Gregorian chants to which religious texts were sung.

Though rare, individual or group singing still spontaneously accompanies the myriad tasks round the house, the yard and in the fields. Lively songs are once again thriving as work songs to accompany tasks related to farming. Naturally, they exist alongside popular songs. Once again, it is customary to celebrate the completion of certain country occupations. Wine-gathering festivals, for instance, have become frequent, and on many state and co-operative farms, a feast is held to celebrate the end of the grain harvest *(Plate 27)*.

End-of-harvest celebrations have ancient traditions in Hungary as elsewhere. Folk song texts referring to the harvest occur throughout Hungary, sometimes combined with ancient pentatonic tunes, more often with new-style melodies, and in a few Hungarian regions which preserve ancient traditions more faithfully, with melodic motifs of some church hymn. (Music Ex. Nos. 14–15).

As has been described, songs connected with special occasions are highly varied with respect to type and longevity. Newer art or popular tunes have replaced the older, simpler pentatonic tunes and those based on old church modes. Undoubtedly, ears grown accustomed to the sound of major and minor scales find the old tunes strange, not only in scale and con-struction, but also in the way they are performed, and this has been a powerful factor in help-ing the new tunes to spread. Young people in particular shy away from them because they are less and less familiar, because their melismata and performance style sound old-fashioned. This process repeats an earlier historical phenomenon. Ever since the Magyars settled in the Danube Basin west of the Carpathians, they were unable to escape European influences.

Whether they wanted to or not, sooner or later they had to adapt themselves to the European cultural community. Nor were they able to avoid being musically influenced. But the pace of change, at first slow and nearly unperceptible, has quickened with time. We have mentioned how significant foreign influences were to Hungarian villages in the 18th–19th centuries, especially after the liberation of the serfs, while in the last few decades an energetic process of equalization has occurred between countryside and city.

Also, as mentioned above, these changes can also be charted in music performed for specific occasions. For a time, the occasion and its customs endure, together with the need for songs associated with it. But these are subject to the law of changing tastes and the desire for the new. The old song is first replaced by a new one, the text of which contains some references to the original occasion. For some time, this serves to link the new tune and text to the special occasion. Even if not durably, the new song and text revive the life-force of the slowly vanishing ceremony that underlies it. Even recently, it has been possible to observe how a textual reference was sufficient to link text and tune to certain special occasions. A song beginning "Twelve are seated at a long table", for instance, which dates from the *Kuruc* times of the 17th century, used to be sung at wedding-feasts because the "long table" became associated with the table of the wedding banquet. The town song beginning "There is a wedding in our street" became popular at wedding feasts because of its text. An earlier bridal dance was ousted by a folk version of an art song beginning "Soon this maiden will become a bride". In the same way, a new-style folk song beginning "Stars, o stars, shine brightly", became linked in certain villages with the firejumping ceremony of Midsummer Eve—this being generally done after sunset.

This leads us to ask whether songs are distinguished in folk-consciousness in terms of old and new. Generally speaking, they are not, but in certain cases the question becomes more complex. In the last sixty or eighty years, the song repertoire of tried and tested individual singers was pretty varied in quality and quantity. In any given village only one or two families, or possibly only one member of the family knew the ballads, and sang them at certain gatherings. The rest of the villagers did not sing them, and some did not even know of their existence, but many people could name the person who was familiar with them. Village singers will often say: "This is a new song"; or "This is certainly very old, I learned it from my grandmother". But it is soon obvious that the opposite is the case, i.e., the song regarded as "new" is the older, and the composer of the one held to be old is known to the collector. It was in

1874 that Elemér Szentirmay wrote the song beginning "There is only one beautiful girl in the world" ("Csak egy szép lány van a világon"), which became famous through the folk play "The Village Villain", and was played by gypsy bands not only within Hungary but also among the neighbouring peoples. Furthermore, "I was at the plucking last night" (Tollfosztó-ban voltam este) was sung in spinning rooms at the turn of the century as a folk song to a popular art song melody. As Bartók put it, "the art song turned into a true folk song, firmly shaped and vigorous."

It often happens that a song performed by an old man in an old-fashioned manner is regarded as "old", but performed in a youthful style, it is considered "current". Good singers regard the same melody as another song if it is sung with a different text. It has always been very typical of village musical life—and still is—that songs regarded as old, or old-fashioned, disappear in the mists of oblivion, but can just as easily become fashionable again. It has been possible to observe this happening in the life of new-style songs during the last few years. Often, forgotten songs come back into fashion through the radio.

Earlier researchers maintained that traditional life in the country was dominated by a rigid outlook, fixed religious convictions and tastes, and an unchanging, uniform way of thinking. This was equally binding on every member of the community, determined by unwritten laws, and sanctioned by the strength of tradition. It would be a great mistake to regard this as a valid conclusion for the village of today, or even of a hundred years ago. The closer we come to the present, the fewer are the traces—and ultimately even these are gone—of such former conditions. Yet the transformation is very slow and goes through any number of gradations. The customary does not vanish all at once; traditions and customs still retain great significance in highly differentiated communities.

Homogeneous folk song styles can evolve and endure only in homogeneous, or only slightly differentiated communities. In societies of increasing complexity, however, these closed communities disintegrate. Changing conditions of life in the socio-economic sphere, and a transformation of life, thought and habit, do not tolerate rigid, immutable forms. That is why the new style evolved and eclipsed the old style, and how pentatonic songs became for-gotten. No statistical data exist on the survival of the new style, but musical influences from the city appear to gain ground in the villages in direct relation to the appearance of new oppor-tunities for work, new forms of community life and new forms of entertainment—in short, in relation to the extent that differences between town and countryside decrease.

Whatever the role of the new style, the old-style songs will remain eternally of historical value and significance, together with a third group not classifiable under a single heading. Hungarian folk music has been preserved for the nation and given a fitting place in relation to Hungarian art music. Bartók maintained that the first results of research into peasant music ensured a firm basis for a rapid development of contemporary art music. The guiding influence of folk music on Hungarian composers has been all the stronger, in that they have also been in the vanguard of folk music research.

Béla Bartók also explains how the influence of folk music can operate in art music: "First of all, an entirely unchanged, or only slightly varied, peasant tune is provided with an accompaniment, and possibly with a prelude and postlude... This kind of folk song elaboration can be done in two ways, one passing over into the other without a precise dividing line. In one, the accompaniment and the prelude, postlude or interlude are only of secondary importance... In the other, it is just the reverse: the peasant tune becomes a motif, and the main thing is what is placed around and under it... Sometimes the influence of peasant music shows itself as follows: the composer does not make use of real peasant tunes, but, instead, invents some sort of imitation of a peasant tune." In yet a third method, the composer neither elaborates nor imitates a folk song, "yet his music distils the same atmosphere as peasant music. It is then true to say that the composer has learned the musical language of the peasant and has mastered it as perfectly as a poet masters his native language". The lifework of Béla Bartók, Zoltán Kodály and László Lajtha all bear this out.

FOLK INSTRUMENTS

For many centuries, several instruments occupied an important place in Hungarian musical life. Documents dating from the earliest centuries following the settlement of the Magyar people in their new home (A. D. 896) have preserved a number of personal names and places directly associated with the musical instruments of those times. The earliest recorded were the names *Kürtös* (horn blower) and *Sípos* (piper), and then, with ever-increasing frequency, *Gaydos* (droner), *Dudás* (bagpiper), *Dobos* (drummer), *Trombitás* (trumpeter), *Hegedűs* (fiddler), etc., indicating that the number of instruments likely increased as well as the names, and that the instrumental inventory developed not only in the royal court but in other parts of the country as well. A list of words from about 1390 already contains numerous Hungarian names of instruments. Chronicles from those times describe the musicians in King Matthias's court. In later centuries, countless varieties of entertainers and comedians came into existence, all playing at least one, if not more, musical instruments. *(Plate 5)*. The number of orchestras on aristocratic estates greatly increased, and feudal lords rivalled one another in acquiring this or that famous violinist, bagpiper or trumpeter.

There are no exact data as to what musical instruments were in use amongst the general population before the 18th century, but judging from certain references and illustrations, they must have been familiar with the instruments of the aristocratic orchestras, even if they did not use them, particularly as musicians were drawn from amongst the serfs. The instruments most in use in the villages were those which anyone could fashion with a little experience and simple means. The folk instruments of the past 100 or 150 years have been preserved through practice and memory. They even include instruments that came into use during the last couple of centuries. By the same token, it is also quite likely that one or two instruments, known and used in former years, have been forgotten.

Research into Hungarian folk instruments, like regular folk song collecting and the systematic study of Hungarian folk music, is linked to the names of Béla Bartók and Zoltán Kodály. The swineherd's horn and bagpipe were first described by Béla Bartók in 1911 and

1912, respectively; later, Zoltán Kodály described peasant instrumental music and folk instruments in his study of Hungarian folk music. The work of these two pioneers has been continued by researchers whom they have trained, and who have supplemented their work with their own investigations.

The study of folk song and folk instruments forms an integral part of Hungarian historical and ethnographical research. Their characteristics and transformations mirror the changes that have taken place in musical life of the Hungarian people. They reflect its long history, work, griefs and joys, and throw light on the recesses of its everyday life, which cannot be penetrated by means of the meagre data of ancient documents and chronicles. Hungarian folk tunes and instruments mark the road travelled by our ancestors and bear witness to what Hungary has been able to contribute to world music.

In the following pages, I will describe only those instruments capable of playing tunes (with or without a text) in use during the last century and a half, which were made by their users or by some member of the community. Instruments made by professional craftsmen are not included even if they have been significant in the musical life of the peasantry.

THE SHEPHERD'S FLUTE

An internationally-known instrument, the shepherd's flute, was widely adopted in Hungary *(Plate 14)*. The old proper name *Sípos* (flutist) suggests that this instrument was used from the beginning of the 12th century. The instrument was possibly not the same as the shepherd's flute of today, but it is certain that the common Hungarian word for flutes "pipe", as for example, the willow-pipe, did mean some kind of flute. In short, the word "pipe" has been commonly used to designate the shepherd's flute. The herdsmen in Hungarian Nativity plays mention both the pipe and the shepherd's flute. In his memorandum on Transylvania, written in the first half of the 18th century (a document also important from an ethnographic point of view), Péter Apor writes: "fiddle, cimbalom and bagpipe being at hand, they were often joined by the shepherd's flute".

Recent research has not been able to ascertain whether the shepherd's flute was used in an ensemble of instruments. It is recorded as a solo instrument, and in the past it was used by peasants and herdsmen. But in the last sixty or eighty years it has been used only by herdsmen, who not only know how to play it but make it with great skill. At the turn of the century, forests and fields echoed with the sound of this flute. Shepherds were particularly fond of it. More than one aged herdsman boasted that even ladies of rank stopped to listen to the sound of his flute playing in the forest. Sometimes a girl would become the wife of some young herdsman because he played so beautifully.

A herdsman flutist often owned three or four instruments. He always took at least one of them with him when he was grazing his herd. Some of the herdsmen even made cases for their instruments. In Transdanubia, the fipple section was protected from the dust and soil by a leather cap. The herdsman kept his instrument either in his knapsack, or in the sleeve of his long cloak. When the herd was quietly grazing or resting, the herdsman would take out his flute and play it. When two herdsmen met, they compared flutes and even sometimes exchanged them. If they happened to meet at a roadside inn and were in a good mood, they might dance to the music of the shepherd's flute, if there were no bagpipes or a gypsy band.

The making and playing of flutes was handed down from father to son, from elder herds-man to younger, often to a boy as young as ten. The boy would watch over the flock with his amster, the head shepherd. The boy learned how to make and play the instrument, how to blow it, to place his fingers over the holes and to choose and carve the branches needed for making it. Some older herdsmen were very good teachers. The lesson always began with learning to play a song on the flute.

The favourite wood for making the pipe was elderberry, available throughout the country. A branch of suitable length and thickness was cut and allowed to dry for a few weeks, six months, or even a year, in its bark. Then the bark and pith were removed and, if the internal opening was too small or the wood was too thick, the inner opening was expanded with a suitable borer. Then came the work requiring greater skill, the carving of the hole—often referred to as the "beaver-hole"—situated just behind the mouthpiece. This was followed by the insertion of a stopper called a "tongue", and a note would result if the beaver-hole had been well carved. If the tone produced was pleasant, pure and penetrating, the drilling, or burning of the finger-holes with a hot iron would follow. Some herdsmen patterned their flutes after an existing model, while others simply used their fingers for measuring the flute's length, its thickness, the distance of the beaver-hole from the upper end of the instrument, and the distances of the finger-holes from each other. When all this was done, tuning followed. Holes producing too deep a tone would be widened with a knife or a hot iron.

Although some herdsmen had exceptional skill in playing and making these flutes they were rarely naturally in tune. A good player, however, still managed to play in tune by adjust-ing the intonation with fingerings. During the last hundred years, two kinds of shepherd's flute were widely used in Hungary: one was a six-hole flute of various lengths, and the other was the Transdanubian five-hole type, known as the "long flute" (hosszi furugla), from 80 to 100 cm long. Although folk museums in Hungary preserve other types as well, they quite prob-ably came from neighbouring peoples. A tune-octave major scale plus a major third can gen-erally be played on the six-hole type. The lower octave can be played by blowing gently, the second octave by overblowing, and the fundamental tone and the major third of the third octave can be obtained by blowing more strongly.

The fundamental notes of six-hole flutes naturally depended on their lengths. The shorter they were, the higher they sounded; the longer they were, the deeper the pitches. Their lengths normally varied between 30 and 60 cm. For instance, the fundamental note of a pipe 35 cm long was B below middle C, one 45.5 cm long sounded the F below middle C. As mentioned earlier, a good player could play perfectly in tune by means of certain fingerings. If he wanted to play a minor tune in the scale beginning with the fundamental note, he had to alter the major third to a minor third. Many shepherd's flutes can play a "neutral" third. The interval of the third (the third note of the scale) was sounded by leaving open the second finger hole from the bottom; this is either a major or a neutral third. If the player wanted to alter the major third to a minor third, he would half cover the hole, or cover the hole below it, that is, apply cross-fingering. He would use cross-fingering or cross-positioning in other cases too, if he felt the need for it. Poorer players did not often feel any need for this, and their intonation suffered as a result. The intervals were not exact; they would play a minor third in place of a major third, or vice versa. But because of incorrect blowing, the harmonic would often sound instead of the note intended.

The player of the shepherd's flute played the same tunes that were sung in his community. If he regarded certain tunes as difficult or was not used to playing them, he would say: "This is no good on the flute." And if he did not know the fingerings for certain notes, he would say: "This flute doesn't have these notes." Naturally, real artists were also to be found amongst flute players. In recent years, elderly players could still be heard playing a few of the old-style pentatonic songs, as well as new-style and other songs. But the number of players has rapidly declined. The herdsman's life has been transformed, the herdsmen have been replaced, and their children no longer even handle the instrument, regarding it as an old-fashioned relic of a vanished way of life. At the turn of the century, any number of good shepherd's flute players were to be found everywhere in the country, but nowadays they may be counted on two hands.

Side by side with the shepherd's flute, there existed folk version of the Western art music transverse flute but without keys. This was called the *flajta,* or *flóta,* after the word *flauta,* and was also known as the "side-flute". Most often this, too, was made of elderberry, but it could also be made out of maple of pearwood. The length varied: generally it was shorter than the Western flute, but longer than the piccolo. Apart from the method of blowing, the playing technique and repertoire were the same as for the shepherd's flute. Some shepherds would play both flute types.

The long flute mentioned above, 80–100 cm in length, only occurs in Transdanubia where it used to be played by peasants as well, though at the turn of the century mostly herdsmen

Berzence, Somogy County

played it *(Plates 12* and *13)*. It, too, was usually made of elderberry. Its length and its five finger-holes distinguish it from the short shepherd's flute. Since these finger holes are placed at the far bottom end of the flute, the performer has to hold his head back and extend his arms at full length to cover the holes. The growling voice of the performer nearly always accompanies the deep tone of the instrument.

Players with artistic inclinations would ornament their instruments. Engraving, etching and, in Transylvania, inlaying with sealing-wax were the oldest techniques, later followed by embossed carving. The designs would include lines, rings, teeth and geometrical patterns. The engraving was done by etching thin lines with the point of a sharp carving knife. The fine scratches were then rubbed with some kind of black grease to make the lines more distinct. Floral designs, birds, human and animal figures were drawn with the engraving tool. When sealing-wax was used, an effort was made to depict scenes in colour. Sealing-wax would fill up the outlines, the narrower and wider lines of the drawings. Sometimes the spaces between the decorations were deep carved, then filled with wax. It was applied in a molten state with a heated metal implement, often the handle of a spoon, which was used to press the wax into the grooves. Recently, embossed carving has become more popular. Some flutes are real masterpieces of the herdsman's art.

THE REED PIPE AND THE BAGPIPE

Over the centuries, it is probable that no instrument played a more significant part in Hungarian life than the bagpipe *(Plates 10, 11, III, IV, V)*. It was played by herdsmen, peasants, soldiers, miners and townsmen. It was used in the orchestras of the aristocracy, and, for a time, it was included in the developing gypsy bands. Long ago, a bagpiper would play music for dancing, and accompany the singing at christening, birthday and wedding celebrations, in the spinnery, at pig-killing feasts, and on other festive occasions. Soldiers would spend their leisure time listening to the bagpipe. It was also played at balls in the castle, and at local peasant dances. Bagpipe music also represented the homage of the shepherds to the Christ-child in the Nativity plays.

There are numerous folk tales of witchcraft and superstitious beliefs about bagpipers. Over the course of many centuries, a separate group of folk songs came into existence which peasants called "bagpipe tunes".

But before coming to the bagpipe, we need to describe an instrument related to it, if not in fact its ancestor. This is the reed pipe *(Plate VI)*, an aerophone whose sound is produced by the activation of thin reed flap by air (as in the bagpipe). As its name indicates, it was made of reed. A reed-stem was hollowed out, about 25 cm long and 9–10 mm in diameter. At one end, a tongue was cut in the side; the end of the opening over the tongue was stopped up; and, as in the shepherd's flute, six finger-holes were bored. The reed pipe was then ready. This simple instrument must have been very widely used at one time because even children's sayings mention it:

> I went down into the cellar to pinch some butter,
> My mother came after me to give me a slap.
> I hid amongst the reeds, and made a reed pipe.
> This is how my pipe sounded: dee-doo–doo,
> You're the one with a big mouth.

In Hungary, the reed pipe had a number of variants. One type, different from that described above, had a body made from a separate piece, and a mouthpiece made of reed, inserted into the longer section, which had finger-holes bored in the side. Double reed pipes, resembling the double pipes of the bagpipe, were also made. The two pipes were fitted side by side and tied together. One of the pipes had five holes in front and one at the back, which made it possible to play seven notes of the scale. The other pipe had only one hole. When the hole was open the fundamental note of the reed-stem could be heard, and if covered, a fourth lower. If, for example, the fundamental note was G above middle C, the D below it was sounded. In many parts of the country, boys learned to play such reed pipes when they were between ten and fourteen years old, before beginning on the bagpipe. The single-stem, six-hole reed pipe also played seven notes of the scale. Another type had a seventh hole in the back, higher up than the six in front. This instrument produced eight notes. Its range was from about D immediately above middle C to that an octave above.

These reed pipes survived even longer than their more sophisticated brothers, the bag-pipes. Yet they cannot compare with it in significance, which is why they are not mentioned in old chronicles. Bagpipes, on the other hand, are described in contemporary writings, charters and sketches. In the 13th and 14th centuries, related place and proper names are encountered, such as *Gayd* and *Gaydos*—"bagpipe" and "baspipe". Later, the Arabic or Turkish name *duda* came into general use. Hungarian sources from the 17th century also use the Hungarian term *tömlössíp*, a translation from the Latin *tibia utricularis*.

In the first half of the 16th century, the bagpipe was an extremely popular instrument. It also provided the battle music of the hussars. In 1592, feed was issued for a bagpiper's horse, which meant that he was a military piper who travelled on horseback. It was about this time that the basic types of small instrumental combinations came into existence. The first ensembles were composed of violins and bagpipes, later joined by other instruments. Almost all aristocrats had household orchestras, which included instruments in addition to the bagpipe and the violin: trumpet, *tárogató* (Turkish pipe) *(Plates 6* and *VI/b),* lute, cimbalom, virginals and sometimes the organ, cromorne, trombone and harp. These were played solo or in ensemble.

Ancient chronicles give an idea of the bagpiper's social position. In the early 17th century, a first violinist had an annual stipend of 32 forints as well as the provision of free meals. A second violinist and the bagpiper received 20 forints. The 11 musicians of Prince Ferenc Rákóczi included a bagpiper, one György Dudás, who received in 1666 a cash income of 80 forints as well as earnings in kind: the same, in fact, as that of the virginal player. Only trumpeters and violinists received higher pay—90 forints.

At the end of the 17th century, a great deal was still being written about bagpipers. At carnival time, it was customary for gypsy fiddlers and bagpipers to sit in a sleigh and accompany the sleigh-riders as they made the rounds of the manor houses. Nor was the bagpipe ever absent from christenings, weddings and other festivities of the nobility. But in a description of a wedding feast in 1760, there is no longer any mention of a bagpiper, only the *tárogató*-player, the fiddler, the cimbalom-player, and a new instrument, the *gordon,* a type of "cello", which reproduced the effect of the bagpipe's drone.

In the 18th century, the doors to the West opened wide. With the influx of foreign musicians and new musical instruments, in Hungary, musical life began anew. Instruments of limited range, tune and dynamics like the bagpipe disappeared from the new orchestral ensembles. For a time, it was still in use in gypsy ensembles, but gradually the gypsies abandoned it also. A traveller's journal of 1798 still mentions bands of musicians with bagpipes and cimbaloms, and in 1801 there was a record of a gypsy band with two bagpipers, but after that only bagpipes played by solo performers were still in demand by the village population.

By the end of the 18th century, therefore, the bagpipe no longer had a place in the musical life of the wealthier nobility and the town population. It also ceased to be used in army artillery units, appearing in the early 19th century only sporadically, when army recruiting parties appeared in the villages. But it continued to remain an organic part of the peasantry's musical tradition. The second half of the 19th century was again a period of decline, and the music of the bagpipe ceased to satisfy the needs of the peasantry, though for some time, the instrument survived amongst shepherds. By the middle of the 20th century, only the recollections of story-tellers about the playing of bagpipes were left as reminders. The disappearance of the bagpipe and its music is closely connected with the transformation of Hungarian peasant life beginning in the second half of the last century, after the liberation of the serfs; clear-cut divisions of the peasant community appeared, the city exerted growing influence, the pastoral way of life changed, and so on.

Generally speaking, the bagpipe was forced into the background at the turn of the century, and its place as the instrument for village singing and dances was taken by the increasing number of gypsy bands. This process naturally took place at different times in different parts of the country, according to their particular economic, social and cultural development.

Moreover, although Hungarian bagpipes can be described as being generally uniform, it is still possible to group them according to three main regional areas: the Uplands, the Great Plain and Transdanubia.

The Hungarian bagpipe consists of five main parts: (I) the head, which most often depicts a goat's head or, on rare occasions, a ram's head or a man's head *(Plates V, 7 and III)*; (II) the stem of pipe, or "stock", which is fitted into the head like a tap; it is actually a double reed, consisting of two stems of reed or elderberry, capable of producing sounds by means of a tongue-piece; the lower end is lengthened with an appendage to which an animal horn has been fitted, sometimes depicting a pony or a lute; (III) a mouthpiece, through which the air is blown into the leather bag; in bagpipes on the Plain this was called the blower; (IV) the drone, a pipe made up of several pieces joined by mortising; the pieces consist of a wooden stock (or stem) with an animal, metal or wooden horn at the end, into which is inserted the longer reed or elderberry, producing the deep droning sound with a vibrating tongue; (V) the bag, which is made of sheep, goat or dogskin. When the animal was skinned, the hide was cut only at the hind feet and the head, and pulled whole off body and forelegs, without any cutting in the abdominal part. The skin was then tanned with table-salt and alum, and filled with a bagpipe head in the neck; the mouthpiece was inserted in the place of the right front-foot, and the drone in the left front-foot.

The Hungarian bagpipe produces three notes simultaneously, two through the double pipe, and one through the drone. In front of the stock of the double pipe are five large holes, and a small one above the fifth, called the "flea-hole". Behind this flea-hole, on the back side of the stock, is another large hole. Using the six large holes combined with certain kinds of fingering and a strong blast, eight notes can be played: the scale may be described as "hard" or major, and consists of the fundamental note and the upper octave. By leaving the flea-hole open, the note below is a semi-tone in pitch, which makes it suitable for modulation and for producing a vibrato. The other stock has only one hole. When this is left uncovered, the same note is heard during the blowing as in the stock beside it with all holes covered. When the hole is covered, the note produced is a fourth lower than the fundamental note. That part of the stock containing the five-plus-one large holes and the small flea-hole may be described as the "chanter", because the bagpiper plays his melody with it. The other part, described by bagpipers as the "contra", may be called the contra-pipe, since the covering and uncovering of the one hole produces a repetition of two notes. The third note is produced by the pipe with the vibrating tongue known as the "drone" (or bourdon pipe). This note sounds one or two octaves lower than the fundamental notes of the chanter and the contra-pipe. The total sound is produced in all three pipes by the tongues vibrating from the compressed air blown into the leather bag. On the next page there is an example of a melody performed on the bagpipe.

The bagpipe survived longest amongst herdsmen in the hill-country in the north of Hungary *(Plate 8)*. Here, in a few of the poorer villages, the bagpipe continued to provide the music for weddings, carnival and children's dances right up to the years following the First World War. In the early 1950s, in the hill district of Nógrád County, there still lived about eight or ten bagpipers, who some ten years earlier had played bagpipes while tending their herds out in the fields, or at home, at weddings, carnival dances, and on the streets at Christmas Eve. Today, barely one bagpiper can be found in this area. The bagpipe has gone out of fashion even more than the shepherd's pipe. The generation born after the turn of the century no longer took pains to make and play the instrument, which involves the mastery of many skills. In the 1950s, the Nógrád pipers still spoke of them a great deal.

Mezőkövesd, Borsod-Abaúj-Zemplén County, 1938. Recorded by Bartók

Péter Lukács, former swineherd who was born in 1894 and grew up illiterate, learned bag-pipe playing from listening to his fellow herdsmen. He acquired his first bagpipe from a rela-tive and practised at length in the fields, while watching his pigs, and at home in the evenings. Before long, he was playing for dances in the surrounding region. He even made a number of bagpipes. He used dog skins for bags. He carved the chanters out of plum-wood, and mea-sured the distances between the holes with his fingers. He cut the tongues out of reed. He spoke about the great patience and skill required to tune the pipes. He described how the ton-gue could be shortened or lengthened to produce lower or higher sounds, how the reed could be pushed further in or pulled further out of the stock and how the reed openings at the end of the chanter or contra-pipe—or, for that matter, the finger-holes—could be altered with wax.

Mihály Bertók, born in 1877, was a shepherd until he was eighteen. Later he went to work in a mine. He never went to school, and by the age of twelve or thirteen he was already help-ing his older brother as a shepherd-boy. He was given a pipe-stock by one of the swineherds, which he learned to play. In those days there were still a number of famous bagpipers amongst the shepherds and swineherds. Many times he listened to their playing and watched them as they made their bagpipes, particularly the pipe-stock. In his lifetime he made a great number of instruments, and quite often sold them. In tuning the chanter or the drone, he assembled the instrument, seized the bag by the head, took the mouthpiece in his mouth and the stem of the drone in his right hand, twisting it so that the air would not escape through it while blowing (Plate 9).

Filling the bag full of air, he placed the drone-stock on his right arm or between the horns of the head. If he was deeply immersed in playing, his head and body swayed to left and right with the rhythm of his tune, and occasionally he would squeeze the bag with his left arm. He held the mouthpiece with his teeth, and when he was in the mood he would let it out of his mouth to sing, or sometimes to shout. Sometimes he would drink while playing. At such times, he would let go the stock with his right hand to grasp the wineglass, holding the stock in his left, and letting only the fifth sound, together with the fundamental note of the contra-pipe and the drone.

Peasants remember hill-country bagpipers as being, without exception, herdsmen. Although bagpipe music was an organic part of the peasantry's musical life, only herdsmen played it in this region, and it was regarded as a paid occupation, a vocation for herdsmen. The bagpiper's social standing was different because of his work, and the bagpipe was bound up with it, so that especially well-to-do peasants would have considered it beneath them to play it. Here, as in other regions, the bagpiper often had the reputation of being eccentric or odd, a man who was versed in superstitions. Herdsmen were thought to consort with the devil and to cast spells; they were also supposed to know how to cure sick people and animals.

In recent years, there has been no trace of bagpipers on the Plain, and the instrument itself can only occasionally be found in museums *(Plate III)*. There was a bagpipe tune, well-known in these parts, which began: "Bagpiper, bagpiper, my dear musician…", and every region had its own well-known players *(Plate 7)*. Documents in the Reformed Church at Dévaványa show that, in 1799 and 1801, musical entertainment in the parish was provided by the bagpipe. In the same village, a bagpiper and a flute-player were registered in the records for 1848.

Thirty or forty years ago, famous bagpipers on the Plain lived on only in the memories of older people. Here, just as elsewhere, recollections were spiced with folklore. They endowed earlier bagpipers with exceptional qualities and spun legends about their personalities. They said that in the 1860s one of the inns had a piper whose music had the power to wake the dead. The elders spoke of several one-eyed and wandering pipers who were all outstanding performers. They related that, when the hussars came to the market square at Kunhegyes to recruit soldiers, a piper called Gábor Dudás stood out in front of one of the taverns and played his pipe. All the young men gathered around him and ignored the recruiting party. Finally, two soldiers had to escort him to the outskirts of the town so that they could go about their business. It was said of Márton Tulok Balog that he had himself carried by a whirlwind, but when he sat in a cart drawn by six oxen, the oxen could not budge it. Béni Hajrá was called a dogpiper because the bag of his instrument was made of dogskin. One Sunday morning, young herdsmen enticed him into the town of Karcag and danced to his music in front of the famous Lamb Inn. The young men of the town also gathered there and did not go to church. The old women spread the rumour that the devils had first blown his bagpipe full of air, which enabled him to draw the men around him, and caused them to prefer his piping to the ringing of the church bells.

Especially around the town of Szeged, the bagpipes of the Plain differed in many respects from those found in the hill districts. Here, too, the pipers made instruments decorated with the heads of goats or rams, but more often carved heads of young men and women or girls. In Szeged the bagpipe with the head of a painted girl was known as a "Rosie". To make the

45

instrument more attractive, the bag was covered with a separate skin of black lamb with the hair on the outside, or else with coloured cloth, then adorned with ribbons. The air was blown into the bag not with the mouth, but with bellows. The form of the drone-pipe was also different. There was no horn on the drone or on the other pipes. Some bagpipers already made use of a brass pipe as mouthpiece for the stock and tied a reed tongue to it, just as clarinettists had done long ago.

On the Great Plain, bagpipe-playing was not limited to herdsmen. Pipers included labourers, millers and others. Obviously this was a holdover of a 17th- and 18th-century tradition, when the bagpipe played a much more extensive role in social life and was included in instrumental ensembles. There are references in Szeged, Szentes and Kiskunfélegyháza to the bagpipe being used with the fiddle, clarinet, hurdy-gurdy and cimbalom.

The bagpipe played as important a role in Transdanubia as in the hill districts and on the Plain. The Hungarian poet Sándor Kisfaludy attended a wine-gathering festival at Badacsony in 1795, and mentioned the bagpipe in a poem about the festival. A Transdanubian song about the wedding of Cana of Galilee also refers to it in its last verse: "Good wine without a bagpipe is as foolish as a dance without any leaps." Gergely Czuczor, an early 19th-century poet who wrote a number of verses which became well known as folk songs, noted that Transdanubian herdsmen played either the bagpipe or the shepherd's pipe, and that their singing was a grumble, like the sound of the bagpipe. There was a time in the second half of the last century, and sporadically even later on, when bagpipe music was essential for wedding and pig-killing feasts of carnival time. But just as in the hill-districts, the trade of bagpipe-playing belonged to the herdsmen. Old herdsmen, young at the turn of the century, would relate how any herdsman worth his salt had a bagpipe, and sometimes a merry session in a tavern would last three days and nights to the accompaniment of bagpipe music.

The Transdanubian bagpipe closely resembled the type used in the hill districts. It had no bellows; the head depicted a goat's head, but the horns at the end of the pipes were missing. The stock of both contra-pipe and drone ended in a tube with a rim. While in the Uplands, the hair of the hide was turned inward, and on the Great Plain the hide of a lamb with hair turned outward was pulled over the animal skin bag as a protective covering; in Transdanubia it was customary to use the animal hide directly as an air-bag, with its hair turned outward.

This description of Hungarian bagpipes would be incomplete without a mention of the rich tradition of beliefs surrounding the player and his instrument. Popular belief, as we have seen, attributed extraordinary powers to the pipers. A story is told of a shepherd about fifty years old, a bachelor, who one Sunday afternoon tended his grazing lambs outside the village at a spot where the girls usually sang and played games. The girls asked him to play for them. The shepherd was very willing to oblige, but said that they would have to bring him his bagpipe which was hanging on a nail in the sheep-pen. The girls found it but could not take it down from the wall, because a large red cock was perched on top. When they told the shepherd, he sent them back again. When they looked again, there was no sign of the cock, so they brought the bagpipe. They handed it to the shepherd who blew it up, put it on his shoulder, and strolled after the sheep. The bagpipe began to play a tune, all by itself.

Another legend relates how a bagpiper wanted to rid himself of witchcraft. He buried his bagpipe in a field, by the roots of a briar bush, and every seventh year, he spread a clean cloth under the bush. After that, the witches no longer disturbed him. Many years passed. One night, two herdsmen went by, playing their bagpipes. Suddenly, they heard bagpipe music finer than theirs. They proceeded in the direction of the sound. Soon they came to a briar bush, and under it was a little man, the size of a pipe-stock (about the span of the hand), playing a little bagpipe. The little man pledged with one of the herdsmen: "Take me away, take me away." But the man took no notice; the herdsmen continued on their way, and the little man went on playing his bagpipe under the briar bush.

Old bagpipers believed that they could learn about witchcraft at a crossroad, and could also learn to play the bagpipe there. A hired hand, anxious to play the bagpipe, went to a crossroad. There he was told to open his mouth wide and a wasp would fly into it. This happened, and he went home. At home, his bagpipe began to play without his blowing it. He merely had to say what song it had to play, and the music came, because the devil was blowing it, in the shape of an ant crawling up and down the pipes. Two years later the hired hand hanged himself, but someone cut the rope in time to save his life. He reproached his rescuer for not leaving him there to die as he would have had a lovely funeral with twelve red-trousered gypsies to play at it. A year later he jumped into a well.

Numerous legends speak of bagpipers taken to parties and wedding celebrations by witches. Once a piper was making his way homeward from a nearby village some time before midnight. He was accosted by two women who asked him whether he would like to play for them. Of course he would, he replied. He went with the women to play for them for about half an hour. They came to a splendid castle, where tables spread with food awaited them.

When the bagpiper had eaten his fill, he took out his bagpipe, but the women gave him a handsomer one than his own. He played and played while about forty women danced. At midnight, the half-hour was up, and they asked him what they owed him. The piper said they should give him what they felt he deserved. The women reached into their pockets and each gave him a piece of gold. The bagpiper sat down and put away the money with his bagpipe. In the meantime, one of the women breathed on him. This made him so drowsy that he fell asleep. He woke up at five o'clock in the morning, sitting on the top of a tree in the middle of a field. In place of the gold coins his pockets held pieces of broken tile, and, instead of the handsome bagpipe, he found he was holding a dead dog.

Variants of these curious legends also occur amongst Hungary's neighbours. Bagpipes related to the Hungarian types are also found. Often Slovakian bagpipes are identical with the hill-district type. The only difference seems to be the absence of the flea-hole from the Slovakian chanter, and there are brass horns in place of the animal horn at the end of the stock of contra-pipe and drone. The bagpipe tunes are also similar, sometimes with Hungarian and sometimes with Slovakian texts. There seem to be far greater differences between the bagpipe found on the Hungarian Great Plain and the South Slav types of bagpipe. The latter are without goat, ram or human heads, and the double pipes are held together by a simple block. Only six notes can be played on the chanter, as opposed to the eight notes of the Hungarian bagpipe, because the hole in the back is missing. At the end of the contra-pipe is a large wooden funnel for a horn. In parts of Croatia, pipe-stocks with back holes were found, but the seventh and eighth notes were sounded by a separate, third pipe with a vibrating tongue. It is not known when the present-day Hungarian bagpipe evolved, but there is no doubt that its evolution was very closely connected with the rich and variegated crop of Hungarian bagpipe tunes.

STRINGED INSTRUMENTS

Up to the present, the folk instrument most widely used in Hungary has been the zither, or table zither. The instrument can still be found in most villages even if hidden away in some corner of the attic or the larder, often with broken or missing strings. In many parts of the country, it played an important role in village entertainment in the early part of the century. The zither was preferred by adolescent boys, young men and young married couples. Social differences did not restrict its use. Servants at manor houses, village cotters and peasants with small holdings were amongst its players, as well as the sons of wealthy peasants *(Plate 17)*. There were numerous occasions for playing the zither. Young people played a zither to lessen the monotony of long winter family evenings. Older members of the family taught songs to the young people. Groups of young unmarried men would often play the zither. On starry summer evenings and on Sunday, the sound of the zither's plucked strings could be heard. Young people would dance to the zither while spinning, plucking feathers, and on other occasions. On Sunday afternoons, the singing of the girls would mingle with the sound of the zither as they danced in a circle. Some small boy who could play the zither would likewise accompany the wedding-games of little girls.

Nothing is known about the domestic development and spread of the zither, but it clearly owed its popularity to two factors: no particular skill, materials or tools were required to make it, especially in its older form; the melody strings produced a dense tone, and so did the accompaniment strings, tuned in various ways. Dance rhythms could be played very effectively. Perhaps its greatest advantage was that its technique was easy to master. Boys could be given a few lessons by their elders, and within a week or two they would be able to pluck out a few tunes. At first they would only pick out the melody, but later on would strum the accompaniment strings as well. The zither's strings would be tuned for them by older people.

The oldest forms of zither were made of one piece of wood; generally medium-soft or soft wood was used. In certain areas, zithers were made of white poplar. The carving of the old type of zither from a single piece of wood was similar to making a small trough. A piece of relatively dry wood was selected, the right length sawn off and roughly hewn into the form of a plank. Then came the carving of the bottom, the trough-like part, with a chisel and curved knife. The outsides were then planed or carved, so that with the body of the instrument pointed downwards, the thickness of the two sides and the soundbox was no more than six to eight millimetres. Five to ten millimetres of solid wood were left on either end. Metal pegs were driven into one end to hold the strings and, in the other end, tuning pegs were screwed. Between the pegs, metal frets were worked into a finger-board. The spaces between the frets, or "notes", as peasants called them, were copied from another zither of similar length, and the ends of the frets were bent and driven into the wood to hold them fast. The instrument was then strung with purchased steel strings.

Later versions of this plank-shaped zither were not carved out of a single piece of wood in the shape of a trough. Instead, the head was formed of a separate piece of hard wood into which the tuning-pegs were screwed. The other ends of the strings were attached to pegs driven into another piece of wood, the block. The two sides and the top were also individual pieces. The so-called "row of notes", the frets, were either driven into the top covering or into a slat attached to it, five to seven millimetres thick. The side piece and top were generally made of soft wood, while the top piece was often made of pine. Two thick pieces of wire at both ends of the zither served as bridges to support the strings.

On the Great Plain, "horse-headed", "child-headed" and "side-headed" zithers, known as *tambura,* were quite common *(Plates VIII and IX)*. These differed from the type described above in that the side opposite the row of frets was graduated down in stages, and each stage had a carved head in the shape either of a horsehead or a spiral. The heads along the side held the shorter accompanying strings. So-called "bulging" zithers could be seen throughout Hungary—obviously the result of Western influence. One side would be arched out, as in Austrian zithers *(Plates X and XI)*. The top, or "abdomen" of each zither contained a sound-opening consisting of a large round opening, or series of small holes, drilled in a circular shape. In Hungarian-speaking areas, typical zithers were of the type found on the Great Plain, with horse-heads, child-heads, and side-heads. These were rarely seen amongst neighbouring peoples. But the plank-shaped and bulging varieties could be found both amongst Slovaks and Rumanians.

The zithers were of varying lengths, some ranging from 50 to 80 cm long, and even longer. Diatonic zithers were the most common and were found mostly in hill districts and in

Transdanubia. Chromatic zithers came from the Great Plain. The frets of the diatonic zither were in a single row, while those of the chromatic zither were in two rows. Generally three or four strings were strung over the rows of frets of the diatonic zither. The chromatic or semi-tone zither also had four strings strung over the diatonic row of frets, with a further two strung over the supplementary, semitone frets. The diatonic row produced the Mixolydian scale, and the row behind it supplied the semitone intervals; hence, the instrument is known as a "semitone" or "chromatic" zither. The fundamental notes varied with the type of instrument. The note was lower on the longer ones because of the length of the strings. Many zither-players did not even bother to tune them, but were satisfied with any sort of droning sound. Many other players, however, consistently tuned their melody-strings to the accompanying strings. The tuning most commonly found was the fundamental note, its octave, its fifth, a double fourth of the Mixolydian scale, etc. The so-called "guest strings" of the zithers near Szeged were tuned in a common chord, whose fundamental was the fourth note of the Mixolydian scale. The melody-strings of one of the zithers found at Szentes were tuned to the D above middle C, and the melody used a scale built on the fourth degree, the G above middle C. The accompanying strings produced the G an octave higher, G above middle C, D above middle C, G below middle C and its lower octave G.

Zither players usually play in a standing position *(Plate 18)*. Generally, they put the zither on a table, chest or bench, so as to give a stronger, more resonant sound. A player would hold the hammer, sharpened quill or some other piece of horn or celluloid suitable for plucking strings between thumb, forefinger and middle finger. To play the diatonic zither, the plectrum would be held in the left palm and pressed on to the melody-strings with the thumb. To play the chromatic zither, the piece of wood would be pressed with the forefinger, while the middle finger would reach over to the next fret for a note a semitone away. The player would always pull the hammer or plectrum towards him, sometimes plucking only the melody-strings, and sometimes the accompaniment strings as well. Zither-playing has declined in recent years, but in a few place it has been revived.

At one time, gourd zithers *(Plate XIII/a)* and so-called *tamburas (Plate XII)* were popular, well-known folk instruments in villages on the Great Plain. The two instruments differed from each other primarily in the fact that one had a back made out of a gourd, while the other was made of wood. The *tamburas* had pear-shaped bodies with flat tops or bellies that were glued on. The instrument's long neck extended from the body, and, as with the zither, a row of frets, made of pieces of wire, were driven into it. The scale they produced was similar to that of the diatonic zither. They normally had four steel strings. The player would play the melody on two of these, mainly by holding them down with the middle finger of the left hand and by plucking them with the right, as the instrument lay in his lap. Nowadays the gourd zither can only be seen in museums, but there are still some elderly Serbians near the town of Mohács who play the old *tambura*.

The so-called "rotary lute", descendant of the hurdy-gurdy *(Plates XIV and XV)*, was also widely used on a part of the Great Plain, near Kiskunfélegyháza, Szentes, Csongrád and Szeged. As the "lyre", it could also be found amongst Rumanian, Polish and Ukrainian peoples. It is not known when it was introduced to Hungary, where it became widespread. It quite probably came from Italy during the 18th century or, more likely, at the end of the century. Since the making of the rotary-lute required considerable skill as well as suitable wood and tools, relatively few people engaged in the craft. It usually accompanied the violin or bagpipe at wedding feasts, carnival time and name-day celebrations. Both the makers and players of the rotary-lute came from poor sections of the population, mostly day-labourers with little or no land. *(Plate 15)*. Craftsmen would make the instrument during the winter months, when there was plenty of free time. According to János Szerényi, the oldest rotary lute-player in Szentes, this town was the chief centre for the instrument *(Plate 16)*. The best-known maker of the rotary-lute, János Berecz, lived there during the second half of the last century.

In appearance, the rotary lute resembles a cello without a neck. The sound is produced by rotating a wooden disk with a handle against the strings, hence the Hungarian name of the instrument *tekerőlant* or, in English, rotary lute. The wooden disk, occasionally rubbed with resin, served for a bow. The instrument had three or four strings. One of them was the melody-string, while the other two or three played the accompaniment at the fifth and the octave. The instrument used by János Szerényi of Szentes had three strings: the so-called "prime" or leading string, tuned to D above middle C; the so-called "crackling" string, tuned to G above middle C (this string provided the rhythmical accompaniment with a crackling sound produced by the turning disk); and the "drone", tuned to lower G. The melody was played by depressing a series of wooden keys, arranged in parallel and giving two octaves of the chromatic scale. The length of the string was shortened at the desired points by depressing a key, in somewhat the same way as the keys of a flageolet. The keys returned to their original position by their own weight after being depressed. After having fastened the instrument firmly to his body with a leather belt round his waist to prevent it from moving while being played, the player held the rotary lute in his lap and played the keys with the left hand, while turning the wooden disk with the right.

János Szerényi, whose father was also a famous maker and player of the rotary lute, said that he normally played with a clarinettist. In earlier days, the rotary lute was played with a bagpipe. The open melody-string of the rotary lute was tuned to the clarinet in D, but the first key to be pressed was G above middle C. The double-pipes of the bagpiper near Szentes also produced G above middle C as their fundamental note. According to Szerényi, it was always the lute-player who began the tune and the clarinettist who followed him. Other informants, however, said that it was the clarinettist who began, because it was easier to hear its tone in the ensemble than if the tune were played on a rotary lute. The clarinet-rotary lute ensemble played both "tunes for listening" (often *lento* or *adagio* in tempo) and dance tunes. In addition to the slow and quick *csárdás* tunes, polkas were also played on the rotary lute.

THE CIMBALOM AND GYPSY MUSIC

Like most Hungarian folk instruments, the old form of cimbalom was part of the musical life of manor houses and was used in church music as well. Its name first appeared in the *Vienna Codex* in the 15th century, and then in the *Érdy Codex* in the first half of the 16th century. In his work on "infernal spectres" (1578), Péter Bornemissza also mentions the cimbalom. In one of his hymns, Miklós Bogáthi Fazekas speaks of the "sonorous cimbalom". According to the accounts of Nádasdy in 1564, there was a cimbalom-player called Imre in the town of Sopron. György Zrínyi, who in 1596 captured two gypsy fiddlers from the Bey of Pécs, wrote that one "has a cimbalom shaped like the one with which clerics sing mass, but does not strike it with sticks, only plucks it with his fingers, like a harp". A great wealth of documentation indicates that the cimbalom was essential at merry-making.

A narrative poem about Bercsényi's wedding in 1695 gives a lively description:

> Here the cimbalom's strings when struck did twang,
> The virginal's keys more gently rang,
> Many fiddles from skilful bows resounded,
> The bagpipe's drone from the walls rebounded.

In those times, the cimbalom was an integral part of the orchestras of the aristocracy. The members of the household orchestra of Count Erdődy in 1666 included 3 violinists, 1 cimbalom-player, 3 pipers, 4 trumpeters, 1 bagpiper and 1 drummer.

István Gyöngyösi described the orchestra of his period as having a special tune for each course of the wedding-feast:

> Call the fiddler to come with the bagpipe,
> Zither, cimbalom, lute with the virginals,
> Play a tune when they reach the veal...

During the 18th century, flourishing Western art music was beginning to gain ground in Hungary, and foreign musicians came more and more often, bringing with them instruments which were more developed, modern and fashionable. The simpler instruments of the old orchestras survived separately amongst the peasantry: the cimbalom, and for a time, the bag-pipe, survived in ensembles which no longer catered to the aristocracy, but only to the lesser nobility and the peasantry. As János Nagy wrote in the *Nyájas Múzsa* (Gracious Muse) (1790), these ensembles now consisted overwhelmingly of gypsies and their instruments, the fiddle, cimbalom and cello. *(Plates 6, 21, I and II).*

> I will have the cimbalom-player,
> At night he is not sleepy,
> I found two fiddlers,
> And even a bass-player,
> Whether slow, or fast,
> They play the minuet well...

In 1787, Gvadányi wrote in his work *Pöstényi Förödés* (Bathing at Pöstyén) about the five-piece band from Szeredi, which included a cimbalom-player and a doubler. The same ensemble can be recognized in his poem, published in 1791:

> Three put their fiddles to their ears,
> The cimbalom-player put his cimbalom on his knees
> An old man bent himself to his cello...

Although from the 18th century onwards, gypsy ensembles of all sizes composed of descendants of the gypsy fiddlers began to abound in the orchestras of the nobility, it was still quite possible to find orchestras whose members were craftsmen, peasants and even Jews. A cimbalom was always included in these ensembles. It served as a solo instrument among the peasants, and they made the cimbalom and zither themselves. As late as the turn of the century, there were still a few peasant cimbalom-players in the counties of Abaúj and Zemplén, as well as on the Great Plain and in Transdanubia. The cimbalom was used as folk instrument and was known by the same name in Rumania, Banat, Transylvania and Moldavia, as well as in the Slovakian and Moravian regions of Czechoslovakia. It was also found west of Hungary. Apart from cimbaloms found in the county of Veszprém, peasant cimbaloms were no longer in usable condition. The size, shape, tuning and range of peasant cimbaloms varied greatly. Nor were the cimbaloms of the gypsy orchestras all the same. The makers of these instruments included gypsies, peasant farmers, carpenters and other craftsmen. In some provincial towns in scattered regions in the second half of the last century, cimbaloms were still made by specialized carpenters. All cimbaloms had the typical trapezoid form. But they were all a great deal smaller and lighter than present-day cimbaloms with their metal frames. The player always carried his instrument on his back, secured by ropes or leather straps crossed over his shoulders. If he played it while walking, he carried it in front of him, supported from his neck by a strap or cord. When he sat down to play it, he laid it across his knees or put it on a table or barrel, since the instrument had no legs. As old illustrations show, the cimbalom hammers were two specially carved wooden sticks, and the striking ends were bent upwards to avoid their getting caught in the strings. The tone of the cimbalom was much more metallic because it was struck with bare hammers, in sharp contrast to the padded hammer of today. The cimbalom-player used his instrument to play melodies. In a few village bands, some old players still play melodies, only occasionally striking a chord. The modern cimbalom differs from the old in dimensions, structure, tonal range and sound. The instrument now used by gypsy bands—fashionable in households of the gentry at the turn of the century—was developed in the 1870s by an instrument-maker called József V. Schunda from Pest, who provided it with a damper pedal.

Gypsies have always been noted as players of the cimbalom. Chroniclers have left a description of the merry-making that took place in 1543 at the Viennese court of Queen Isabella, where not even Cardinal György Fráter remained aloof from the dancing. The finest "Egyptian" (i.e. gypsy) fiddlers played there. They did not pluck the strings with their fingers, but beat them with wooden sticks, and accompanied this with singing at the top of their voices. In the 17th and 18th centuries, gypsy ensembles were constantly employed, and the cimbalom was one of the instruments most often mentioned as used by them.

Gypsy musicians supplied the music for weddings and parties of both the lesser and middle nobility, as well as for the middle-class section of the town population. Some gypsy musicians, such as Panna Czinka (1711–1772) and János Bihari (1769–1828), became famous throughout the country. Their music, playing style and repertoire had by then become thoroughly adapted to the needs of celebration and entertainment. In 1791, on the subject of ensemble "improvisation" by gypsy bands, the Hungarian poet, Ferenc Verseghy, compared their "impoverished, beat-less pieces of music" with the way villagers would hum sacred or secular songs, and the way that drunkards would walk...

Ferenc Liszt's book *Des Bohémiens et de leur musique en Hongrie,* published in 1859, allowed a great misconception to spread throughout Europe: he alleged that the music played by gypsy musicians was their own and, hence, that it was gypsy music. Liszt regarded their unrestricted, undisciplined and rhapsodic style of performance as their ancient musical heritage. Sámuel Brassai replied to Liszt's mistaken conclusions thus: "The entire instrumental music of gypsy bands," he wrote, "developed side by side with the exaggerated style of ornamentation adopted by the European virtuosos (instrumentalists and singers)... their style of ornamentation is nothing but the gleanings of European virtuosity; its irregularities, which you so glorify, stem not from the independence of the idealised gypsy character, but from the imperfections of botched imitations, which we can observe in every so-called 'natural' musician, be he gypsy or non-gypsy." This style of performance, estolled by many and censured by many, has been preserved by gypsy orchestras. But is should be emphasized that the style of delivery can in no sense be regarded as ancient, as a heritage that the gypsies brought with them from the East, and even less can what they play be described as gypsy. The term "gypsy music" was incorrectly coined, and it was probably this that misled Ferenc Liszt also. What is generally termed gypsy music is a part of Hungarian music.

Anyone who cared to familiarize himself—even as recently as a few decades back—with the repertoire of gypsy orchestras in various Hungarian regions, villages and towns, realized very quickly that it was extremely varied, but was certainly not gypsy. The gypsy musicians of remote villages played melodic material known and sung by the village population, and older gypsy musicians might well remember songs already forgotten by the villagers. When Hungarian village gypsy bands went caroling at Christmastime, they played old-style pentatonic melodies and new-style songs, as well as folk hymns. The musicians of certain districts and villages differed not only in the kind of songs they knew, but also in their style of playing. Their music was in many respects the product of their environment—their village or their region *(Plates 20* and *22).*

The repertoire of gypsy orchestras in the towns was determined by the tastes of the upper middle-class. Gypsy orchestras mainly played art songs composed in folk style, because that is what was requested by this section of the population. Béla Bartók put it as follows: "The music that gypsy orchestras play for money today in the towns is just recent Hungarian art music composed in folk style. The purpose of this type of music in Hungary is to gratify musical needs of a lower order... It is good that 'light music' should spring from a Hungarian speciality... May they retain their ancient repertoire in its oldest garb, and not mix into it waltzes, jazz and what not!"

The spread of radio and television has reduced rural-urban differences. Unavoidably, a growing similarity between the repertoires of urban and rural gypsy bands has developed. Even in the most remote villages, gypsy bandleaders imitate the tunes, harmonies and playing styles heard over the radio. Yet, on the other hand, it is encouraging to see that urban gypsy bands are drawing progressively more on the rich heritage of Hungarian folk music, and that their performance style and harmonies are growing closer to the classical forms of folk music performance.

BIBLIOGRAPHY

A Magyar Népzene Tára *(Corpus Musicae Popularis Hungaricae):*
  I. *Gyermekjátékok* (Children's Singing-Games). Budapest, 1951.
  II. *Jeles napok* (Feast-Days). Budapest, 1953.
  III. *A.—B. Lakodalom* (Wedding Songs). Budapest, 1956.
  IV. *Párosítók* (Matchmaking Songs). Budapest, 1959.
  V. *Siratók* (Laments). Budapest, 1966.
Bartók, Béla: *A magyar népdal* (Hungarian Folk Music). Budapest, 1924.
Bartók, Béla: *Das ungarische Volkslied*. Budapest, 1925.
Bartók, Béla: Hungarian Folk Music. Oxford, 1931.
Bartók, Béla: *Népzenénk és a szomszéd népek zenéje* (Our Folk Music and the Folk Music of
  Neighbouring Peoples). Budapest, 1934.
Bartók, Béla: *Válogatott írásai* (Selected Writings). Budapest, 1956.
Járdányi, Pál: *Magyar népdaltípusok* (Hungarian Folk Song Types). Vols. I—II. Budapest,
  1961.
Kerényi, György: *Népies dalok* (Folk-Type Songs). Budapest, 1961.
Kodály, Zoltán: *Ötfokú hangsor a magyar népzenében* (The Five-Note Scale in Hungarian Folk
  Music). Temesvár, 1917.
Kodály, Zoltán: '*A magyar népzene*' (Folk Music of Hungary). In: A *Magyarság Néprajza*
  (Hungarian Ethnography), Vol. IV., Budapest, 1937. (Followed by revised and enlarged
  editions).
Kodály, Zoltán: *Die ungarische Volksmusik*. Budapest, 1956.
Kodály, Zoltán: *Folk Music of Hungary*. Budapest, 1960.
Manga, János: "Hungarian bagpipers". *Acta Ethnographica* XIV, 1–2 (1965) 1–97.
Manga, János: *Magyar duda—magyar dudások a XIX.-XX. században* (Hungarian
  Bagpipe—Hungarian Bagpipers in the 19th–20th Century). Népi Kultúra—Népi
  Társadalom, 1968.

Manga, János: *Typy gájd v karpatskej kotline*. Acta 1 Ethnologica slovaca (Ph Dr. Jánovi Mjartanovi, DrSc., k 70. narodeninám). Bartislava, 1974. 183–206.

Maróthy, János: *Az európai népdal születése* (The Birth of the European Folk Song). Budapest, 1950.

Sárosi, Bálint: 'Die ungarische Flöte'. *Acta Ethnographica* XIV. 1–2 (1965) 141–163.

Sárosi, Bálint: *Die Volksmusikinstrumente Ungarns*. Handbuch der europäischen Volksmusikinstrumente. Band I. Leipzig, 1967.

Sárosi, Bálint: *Cigányzene* (Gypsy Music). Budapest, 1971.

Szabolcsi, Bence: 'A XVII. század magyar főúri zenéje' (The Music of the Hungarian Aristocracy in the 17th Century). *Zenei Szemle* XII., (1928).

Szabolcsi, Bence: 'Népvándorláskori elemek a magyar népzenében' (The Age of Migrations in Hungarian Folk Music). *Ethnographia*, 1934, 138–156.

Szabolcsi, Bence: 'Egyetemes művelődéstörténet és ötfokú hangsorok' (Five-Note Scales and History of Civilizations). *Ethnographia*, 1936, 233–251.

Szabolcsi, Bence: *Népzene és történelem* (Folk Music and History). Budapest, 1954.

Szomjas–Schiffert, György: 'A finnugorság ősi zenéje nyomában' (In the Path of the Music of the Finno-Ugrians). In the reprint of *Magvető* 3. (1965).

Szomjas–Schiffert, György: *Hajnal vagyon, szép piros . . .* (It is a beautiful red dawn). Budapest, 1972.

Vargyas, Lajos: 'Ugor réteg a magyar népzenében' (The Ugrian Strata in Hungarian Folk Music). In: *Kodály emlékkönyv* (Kodály Memorial Book). Budapest, 1953.

TRANSLATION OF THE SONG TEXTS

1 Fly, O peacock, fly,
  Upon the County Hall
  To bring release
  For many poor prisoners. (Page 12)

2 The coach rattles along, Jancsi cracks his whip,
  Maybe they are coming for me.
  O Mother, Mother dear, who once nursed me!
  How quickly they are taking me away! (Page 13)

3 The heart-cherry is ripening,
  I'll take some to my lover,
  I'll take some to my lover,
  If he is ill, these cherries will cure him. (Page 16)

4 From the east a singing skylark is coming,
  But her eyes are tear-stained.
  Under her wing she's bringing me a letter adorned with roses.
  In it my lover writes me that he loves me not. (Page 17)

5 There's no nicer girl than a Magyar girl,
  No other girls have such slender waists,
  For her waist is slender as a reed,
  And she herself goes after the lad. (Page 18)

6 In Nagyvárad's haven the steamboat has stopped,
  The national colours are hoisted on its top.
  The wind blows them, it blows them homewards,
  Old linemen of the first (regiment) are coming on their leaves. (Page 18)

7 Behind the gardens of Bolhás, Kata,
  How many paths there are, Kata,
  Every lad does make one,
  Through it he goes to his love, Kata. (Page 19)

8 The cart is at the gate,
  It has come for the bride,
  The bride says
  She won't marry—ever. (Page 22)

9 Good-bye, Father, dear Father,
  I must part with you.
  Foreign land, foreign soil,
  Take me in, O take me in! (Page 23)

10 Nice is the nice black lamb,
   Nice is the black-eyed girl,
   So is the dark lad
   With the curly hair.
   Oh, great work of charity!
   Cherished sacrament, miracle of faith!
   Refuge of our lonely earth,
   Star of hope for all sinners! (Page 24)

11 Come on, Pasha, come on, let's go to this quarters.
   Come now, let's have a look at little Jesus in that shabby stable.
   His bed is hay and straw,
   Little Jesus is lying on it,
   Oh, our gracious King, our beloved Jesus! (Page 25)

12 Here we come, here we come,
   St. Stephen's servants!
   According to the old custom,
   We want to know
   What you will give us,

And if we may do regölés.*
When we are let in,
We scuffle in.
Our sandals are birch's bark.
Our trousers are buckwheat's blade,
Hej regö rajta,**
The great Lord
May confer (upon you) that too! (Page 26)

13 St.John had the heavenly fire fed—
Ilona Magyar has fair hair,
Her head is adorned with a wreath of pearls. (Page 27)

14 Reap, my honey, reap,
I'll pay you your pence.
If I should not pay you,
My dearest will. (Page 28)

15 Reap, my dove, reap,
I'll pay you your pences...
Now I have paid your pences
And I have reaped with you. (Page 28)

16 I was at the plucking last night,
My sweetheart also had her eyes open;
She always throws it back at me
Who I speak with through the evening. (Page 28)

* A heathen tradition of singing magical songs at Christmas time to ensure prosperity. The tradition was not suppressed by Christianity. The *regös* used to call at each house of the village and receive gifts in turn.
** The recurring incantatory phrase of the *regölés*.

I. Miklós Barabás: "Arrival of the Bride" (1856)
Oil on canvas
Hungarian National Gallery, Budapest

II. Gypsy band
Mid–19th century. Oil on canvas
Art Collection, Ethnographical Museum, Budapest

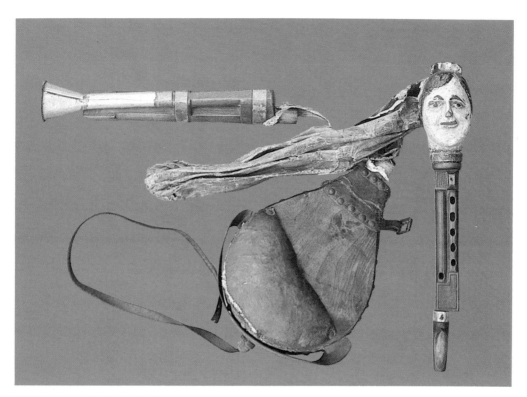

III. Bagpipe with the head of a young woman
Ferenc Móra Museum, Szeged

IV. Palóc lead
ornamented skin pipe
Copy. The original
was made
by András Birinyi

V. Palóc pipe with Tree of Life
motif and mirror ornamentation
on the head
Copy. The original
was made by András Birinyi

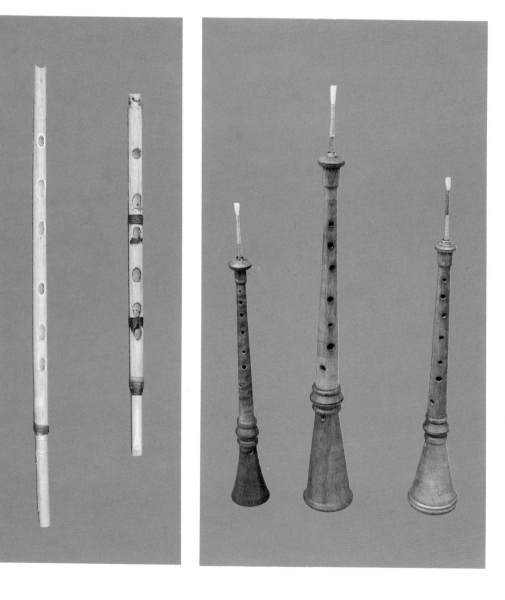

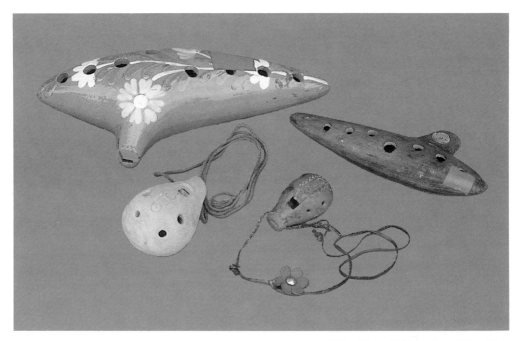

VII/a. Birinyi Collection, Táborfalva

VI/a. Reed pipes
Birinyi Collection, Táborfalva

VI/b. Turkish pipes
Copies based on the collection of the National Museum
Made by József Bige, 1980
Birinyi Collection, Táborfalva

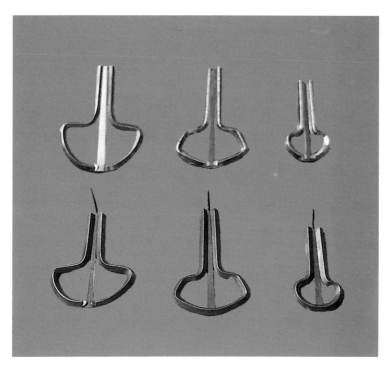

VII/b. Jew's harps
Made by Zoltán Szilágyi, Kecskemét, 1985
Birinyi Collection, Táborfalva

VIII. Zither from the Great Plain with "innerhead" *(tambura)*,
Csongrád, Csongrád County, 1920s
Ferenc Hézső private collection, Hódmezővásárhely

IX. "Horse-headed" zither
Made by János Kanczel, Debrecen, 1967
Birinyi Collection, Táborfalva

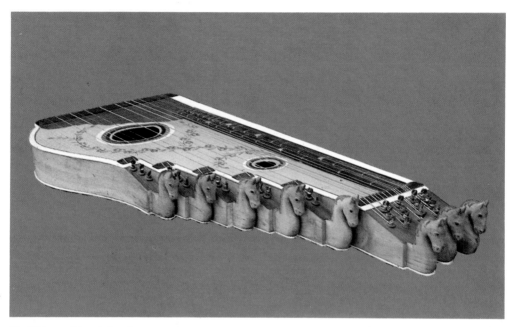

X. Zither with colt heads
Made by Sándor Budai, Sándorfalva, Csongrád County, 1980
Birinyi Collection, Táborfalva

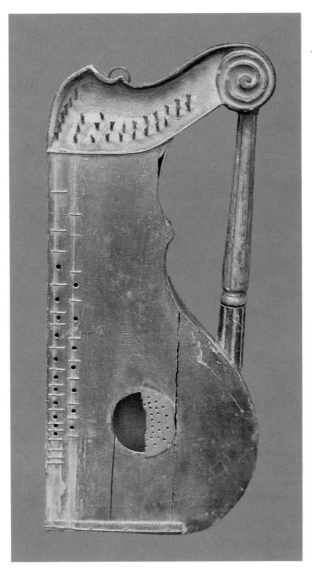

XI. Zither (German model)
Hódmezővásárhely, 1957
János Tornyai Muscum,
Hódmezővásárhely

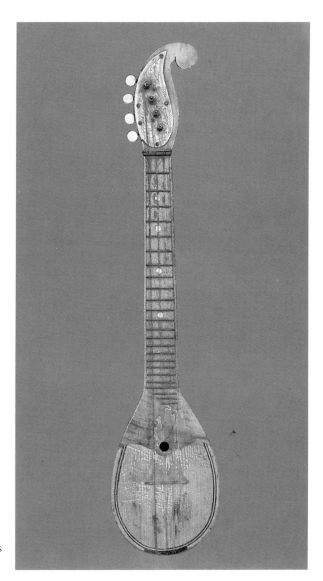

XII. Tambura
Made by a workshop, Budapest, 1920s
Birinyi Collection, Táborfalva

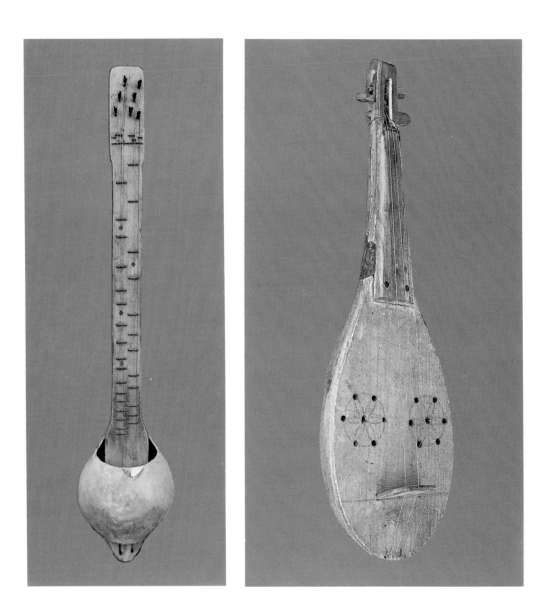

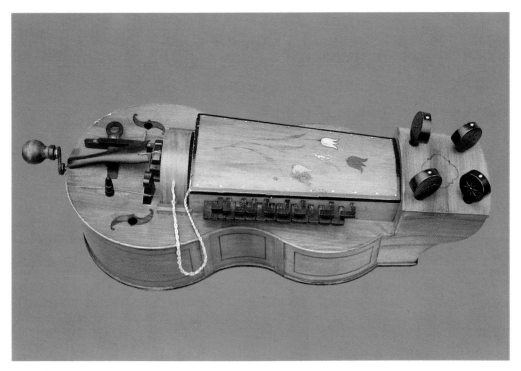

XIV. Rotary lute *(nyenyere)*
Made by Mihály Bársony, Tiszaalpár, 1977
Birinyi Collection, Táborfalva

XIII/a. Gourd zither
Made by András Birinyi, Sr. and József Birinyi, 1979
Birinyi Collection, Táborfalva

XIII/b. Gourd violin
Szeged, Ferenc Móra Museum

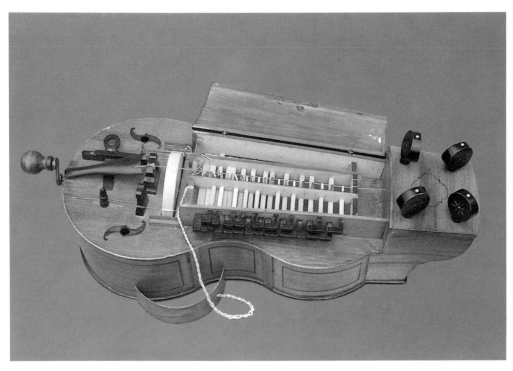

XV. Rotary lute with open sound-box
Made by Mihály Bársony, Tiszaalpár, 1977

1. Man playing the drum and pipe
Győr, County Győr.
Ethnographical Museum

2. Béla Bartók (1881–1945) Budapest, copy of a photograph taken in 1931
Photo Collection of the Ethnographical Archives of the Ethnographical Museum

3. Zoltán Kodály (1882–1967)
Budapest, 1934 Ethnographical Museum

4. Men singing into a phonograph. Behind the table stands folk music collector László Lajtha
Kisgyőr, County Borsod, 1929

5. Collecting folk songs. Young girl sings into a phonograph
Bánffyhunyad, (Heudin, Rumania), County Kolozs, 1902
Ethnographical Museum

6. Recruiting scene with men playing string
instruments, the cimbalom and Turkish pipe
Ethnographical Museum

7. Blowing up the bagpipe Varsány, County Nógrád, 1940
Ethnographical Museum

8. Bagpiper of the Great Plain Orosháza, County Békés, 1920s
Ethnographical Museum

9. Swineherd with bagpipe
Buják, County Nógrád, 1933
Ethnographical Museum

10. Mihály Bertók playing the bagpipe
Kishartyán, County Nógrád, 1933
Ethnographical Museum

11. Herdsmen of the Ipolyság with their bagpipes
Ipolyság, County Hont, 1912
Ethnographical Museum

12. Man playing a long
shepherd's pipe
Alásony,
County Veszprém, 1911
Ethnographical Museum

13. Man playing
the long shepherd's pipe
Bárdudvarnok,
County Somogy, 1932
Ethnographical Museum

14. Shepherd playing the flute
Fadd, County Tolna, 1931
Ethnographical Museum

15. Beggar playing the rotary lute
Budapest, 1934
Ethnographical Museum

16. Dániel Szerényi
playing the rotary lute
Szentes,
County Csongrád,
1950
Ethnographical Museum

17. Young man playing
the zither
Cigánd,
County Zemplén, 1936
Ethnographical Museum

18. Sándor Budai playing a zither of his own making, adorned with a colt's head
Sándorfalva, County Csongrád, 1966
Ethnographical Museum

9. Csángó lad playing
the flute
Lábnyik,
Moldva, Vladnic, (Rumania), 1932
Ethnographical Museum

20. Hungarian band of musicians
Cserépváralja, County Borsod, 1929
Ethnographical Museum

21. The "squeaker band" of gypsy children in Győr, 1897
Győr, County Győr Ethnographical Museum

23. Young men undressing the straw dummy *(kisze)*
by the river Ipoly
Hont, County Hont, 1948
Ethnographical Museum

22. Csángó musicians with violin and cello (ütőgardon)
Gyimes, (Ghimeş, Rumania), 1953
Ethnographical Museum

24. Whitsuntide Queen
Maconka, County Heves, 1931
Ethnographical Museum

25. Girls carrying the straw dummy *(kisze)*
Hont, County Hont, 1948
Ethnographical Museum

26. Fire-jumping on St. Ivan's Day accompanied by the bagpipe
Buják, County Nógrád, 1933
Ethnographical Museum

27. Reapers
Ipolyság, County Hont, 1943
Ethnographical Museum

28. Old women at a wake
Komádi, County Bihar, 1963
Ethnographical Museum

29. Bethlehem players
Pásztó, County Nógrád, 1947
Ethnographical Museum

30. Taking leave of the bride before the wedding
Buják, County Nógrád, 1947
Ethnographical Museum

31. Children's game. *"Kiskomárom, Nagykomárom…"*
Galgahévíz, County Pest, 1947
Ethnographical Museum

32. A grandmother teaching her grand-daughter to dance
Verseg, County Pest, 1948
Ethnographical Museum